MARK TARCHETTI

PICK A LANE

GROWTH STRATEGY IN A FAST-CHANGING WORLD

Alchemy-Rx

Pick a Lane: Growth strategy in a fast-changing world

For information about this title or to order other media, contact the publisher:

Alchemy-Rx
mark@alchemy-rx.com
http://www.alchemy-rx.com

ISBN: 978-1-7353880-0-7 (hardback)

ISBN: 978-1-7353880-1-4 (paperback)

Business / Economics

1 2 3 4 5 6 7 8 9 10

To the strategists...

"All men dream, but not equally. Those who dream by night in the dusty recesses of their minds, wake in the day to find it was vanity; but the dreamers of the day are dangerous men, for they may act on their dreams with open eyes, to make them possible."
–T.E. Lawrence

and

To my One for your support
and love, always in all ways.

To my co-pilot, my coach,
and my team, you each know
who you are. Thank you.

CONTENTS

"IN A WAY, WE ARE MAGICIANS. WE ARE ALCHEMISTS, SORCERERS AND WIZARDS.

WE ARE A VERY STRANGE BUNCH, BUT THERE IS GREAT FUN IN BEING A WIZARD."

-BILLY JOEL

CHAPTER ONE

THE STRATEGIST

There aren't many of us. We are a rare breed. To be good at what we do takes deep and varied experience. We cut our teeth on many different problems as we develop our skills. Embracing change, illuminating opportunity and galvanizing action. We won't accept incrementality or adequacy. Good enough never is.

Career paths for strategists are not easy. Influence is what makes us successful. You don't map neatly to a function. You have to say no to the big operating roles that pack out the standard executive resume. Your seat at the table is an uncomfortable one. You often court controversy in driving for progress. You become the 'forcing function' helping people make the tough choices they would sometimes prefer to avoid – or deal with later. You are the grit in the oyster when times are good, and the passionate believer when confidence drops. You see unexpected potential where others have missed it, finding creative paths to value.

Potential is our purpose.
Transformation is our path.
We believe in the power of building something.
Time is a lens to degrees of freedom.
Resources are a constraint to be overcome.
Progress is our measure of performance.
The future is always an opportunity.
Change is a positive and necessary constant.
What got you here, won't get you there.
We are the strategists. Our passion is your future.

A team that doesn't hunt out their strategist is the weaker for it. The fog of war clouds the day to day in business. We offer a different perspective. Bold ambition, decisive choices, firm steps forward. Strategy is both a skill and a competency. It takes years of experience in many business situations to do it well. At different times a strategist will be dealt strong and weak hands, and must be able to manage them both. We need experience in different types of organizations, from complex corporate portfolios to growth-oriented Founder-led businesses. From these many situations, the veteran learns the tools of the trade. The ability to identify new paths to value. The ability to distill learning from success and failure. The ability to judge the plausibility of a plan. We are rare because there is no established career path. No single stakeholder can provide enough longevity. No one company can offer enough diversity. The best strategists are not theorists but operators and practitioners whose work translates into the implementation of change. Strength in theory is a poor substitute for strength in ideas into action.

Most organizations lack much of what I have just described. They work to the assumption that the c-suite have the time and head space to add sustained strategy work to the bottom of a long to-do list. Despite their title, the annual strategy slide-fests are often anything but strategic. The dark arts prevail. The meetings frequently descend into boardroom lobbying and gaming targets. Through the smoke and mirrors of PowerPoint Promises, presenters exhaust the audience, stifling strategic substance and playing for time. Leaving the room with your plan intact is mission critical. To get to the point would miss the point.

Equally, strategy is not a special project for a handful of off-site meetings. The biggest decisions need depth and detail. Time horizons are longer. Constraints are reimagined. It is exhausting more than it is entertaining. It's a challenging balance of left and right brain, logic and magic. It unites and divides management teams as big ideas are evaluated and debated. Ultimately choices have to be made. Choices for the good of the whole, not for an individual piece. The big picture is a big undertaking.

Many organizations overlook the strategist entirely, tagging the title onto staff roles. This is often strategy in name only. Staff roles are normally filled with political animals, in place to ensure the smooth workings of the CEO office. They manage emotions as much as actions. The strategist by contrast is apolitical but can only succeed with influence. Apolitical influence only comes from impact. Strategy requires an ability to shape the biggest ideas and choices of the organization. Transformative strategy necessitates significant re-allocation of resources without succumbing to the perils of organizational democracy. Change means confronting the objective reality of the capabilities in a business without giving in to faint praise. Some of the biggest investments in strategy are inorganic, buying businesses or acquiring capabilities. The strategist must drive these discussions and should be one of the most critical executives to the organization. The #2 of tomorrow, just as the COO is the #2 of today.

Many of the examples of c-suite strategists are Founder-based. Inventors and innovators who become operational CEOs after initially creating the business. As the business matures and scales, they retain the hot seat to keep control of things. The field of operations is often not their passion, nor does it hold their attention. These Founders demonstrate why strategy and operations are distinct. They often wish they'd stayed the master of ideas. They find the operational challenge and lack of free time in the CEO role limits their abilities to shape the company. The irony of strategy is if you try to do it as the #1, you lack the time and degrees of freedom you need. The superpower of the CEO is a myth and their time is not their own. Stakeholder expectations and institutional tasks dominate their calendar. The operating rhythm, customer meetings, supplier meetings, board meetings, investor meetings, employee engagement, managing the leadership team, governance. The list goes on. The best CEOs recognize these constraints on their time. They embrace the delegation of strategy as the best way to develop the next generation of ideas.

"Strategy is about designing and building better."

It is in these situations that the strategist finds their patron. The patron sets the brief and creates context and permission for the new vision and new ideas. The strategist then plays the role of architect, translating the patron's dream into a tangible reality. This is not just about the big picture. It certainly takes vision, but it needs much more than that. It also takes precision engineering, careful selection of materials and master craftsmen to undertake construction and create the new reality. The best strategists design and plan in detail. They understand the resources and skills needed in the team. They understand handover points and the appropriate limits of each role. They accept the need to deliver on time and budget, making trade-offs as required. They help the patron realize the best version of their dream within the prevailing constraints.

This reinforces why the best strategists are practitioners not theorists. Successful execution is what makes all the difference. Visionary ideas alone are not enough. They must be complimented with detailed plans for execution, building the required capabilities and prioritizing resources in the pursuit of objectives. The most common criticism of the strategist is the tension of short-term results. A lack of energy for big ideas can be seeded in businesses where execution is not sufficiently valued or stable enough to support major change. Unless strategists are realistic about the cadence of change and the cultural development required, even the most brilliant plans will fail. As Drucker said, "Culture eats strategy for breakfast".

Here's the rub. For many organizations, strategy is just an occasional project. The focus of one or two off-sites for fresh ideas and some team building. When the pressure is on, strategy is the first thing to be deferred in favor of tactical responses. The urgent wins over the important in many boardrooms every day. I have been stunned to see how much human and financial capital is spent on maintenance activity with all the resulting wasted potential. Some will even tell you that strategy is execution. If you are unfortunate enough to hear this, do not work for these people. The world is changing faster than many companies can react to and much of the reason for this is a lack of architects. Maintenance teams have taken over many brands and corporations. These are managers not leaders. They see the world incrementally. They spend a great deal of time fixing urgent problems, and progress is measured by delivering the same for a little less cost every year. Victory is declared when bonus targets are hit. Success is a short-term yardstick. The perils of corporate democracy abound. Everyone keeps the resources they've always had. Capability development is often prisoner to individual functional agendas in larger organizations and entirely absent in smaller businesses.

FRESH THINKING AND NEW PATHS TO VALUE ARE NEEDED TO WIN IN THIS DYNAMIC ENVIRONMENT.

Many organizations choose to look outside for help on strategy. First stop: academia with fond memories of MBA classes where leaders dreamed of the roles they now occupy. A vast library of case study thinking turns strategy into stories (polished, post-rationalized, and usually with a hero). The supporting cast of frameworks and systemic models look for homogeneity of approach, linear thinking and predictable results. All logic, little magic. The world is only that simple in short time frames. That's why one year's case study is often next year's turnaround problem.

Then come the consultants. These are vast commercial organizations. Their cost structure forces them to turn strategy into a product that can be delivered by inexperienced associates working all night. Billable hours mount; initiatives become more complex. While the anthill grows, the senior partner focuses exclusively on the CEO and a handful of key stakeholders. They use high-level case studies to demonstrate bold moves in bite-sized chunks. These become a form of peer pressure to tempt CEOs into simplistic changes that become the definition of assignment success. This business model divides and disempowers the team and fails to build culture and capabilities. If the turnaround fails, management can always be blamed. Dependency on outside help is nurtured to drive repeat business.

WE HAVE MUCH TO LEARN FROM THE PURPOSE, PERSISTENCE AND PASSION OF FOUNDERS.

It doesn't have to be this way. I have seen the transformation that is possible in people, market share, market size and profitability when a business makes decisive choices and executes well. While I have worked with some of the world's most accomplished corporate executives, I have also had the privilege to work with many Founders who built very successful businesses. Their stories are inspiring. At their core is always persistent purpose, hard work and a constant process of learning and adaptation. Challenges in uncharted waters were met with passion and clarity of purpose. Simplicity came from focus on the goals that mattered. When every penny counts, this inevitably means money goes to the most important things. Every obstacle overcome makes the team stronger. This is what the Founders I partnered with stood for. They were some of the most strategic leaders I ever worked with. Just as I have done, companies can learn a lot from successful Founders.

Change is upon us. The model that created value in the last 20 years is maturing and breaking down. Companies have designed out the capacity to change and now face a fast-changing world. After nearly two decades of cost cutting, in-house capabilities are limited. An uncomfortable number of businesses have operated in steady state mode for a decade or more, using cost savings and financial levers to deliver a little more for a little less every year. These playbooks have been well rewarded. Success has been enhanced by increasingly levered balance sheets fueling increased dividends and share buybacks.

The perceived wisdom was that big brands could deliver stable cash flows forever, impervious to consumer and customer dynamics. Few imagined that markets could change enough to undermine the unspoken cash cow strategy. Cost savings at the expense of the customer and consumer could proceed without consequence. Portfolios and SKU complexity were reduced and supply chains were re-built around product and packaging homogeneity to fuel margins. Meanwhile, online sales developed and created infinite aisles. The consumer welcomed this explosion of choice and a new generation of insurgent brands were launched in their thousands.

THE GAP BETWEEN WINNERS AND LOSERS IS GOING TO INCREASE.

The same market drivers that sustained stability are now pivoting to promote change. Organic growth is at a 20-year low and is almost zero in the developed world. The gap between winners and losers is going to increase. Successful companies will win by adapting to accelerating trends faster than their peers.

At the end of 2019, the Gartner quarterly risks survey ranked strategic planning assumptions as the top risk facing companies. Executives believe more than half of the time their teams spend on strategic planning is wasted, and the quality of the resulting plans generally falls short of expectations. This is because the assumptions made during the strategic planning process are often outdated or incorrect before execution.[1]

I have spent most of the last decade in the c-suite as the strategist with operating responsibility for building the levers of future growth. This book is in many respects a personal story of my experience and ideas but also my "why". Times are changing. Strategists have never been more necessary. Organizations need to look deeply at the risks and opportunities of change and position themselves for a different future.

This is not like many other business books. Often in this genre, the author has one idea and uses case studies to repeatedly illustrate this idea. This book takes a different approach, outlining what is maturing and breaking down in the business model of the last 20 years and what is changing in underlying market drivers. It covers the past orthodoxies and entrenched cultural wisdoms that will need to be adapted or overcome. It lays out a framework for growth strategy – a dynamic path to re-appraising your business opportunity. This framework explains how to develop an activity based, multi-year plan to unlock your potential within the constraints of time, cost and capability development.

The best strategists judge themselves on outcomes not concepts. Strategy as theory is academia; strategy in practice is about designing and building better. Action not anthills. Projects not PowerPoint. That's why this book is called *Pick A Lane*. Don't wait for perfection. What matters most is forming a point of view on the future and acting decisively to position yourself to win.

**PICK A LANE.
BUILD A PLAN.
MAKE IT HAPPEN.**

CHAPTER TWO

TWO DECADES, TWO BOOKENDS

As I look back at the last 20+ years, I realize my career has been bookmarked by a growth crisis at either end of the timeline. I joined Unilever straight from college in 1997. A graduate trainee in their Finance function with big ambition and little experience. I knew I didn't want to do numbers forever, but I wanted to know what made businesses tick. Finance seemed a good place to learn. I had been told in my final interview that Unilever was no place for the "son of a car park warden," which only made me more determined to make my mark on this incredible institution.

As it turned out my early years were spent living through a growth crisis in the consumer goods industry. What caused the crisis seemed, on the face of it, nothing to do with our business. We were good at what we did. We had leading brands. We diligently measured our performance against competitors and were quick to flex our muscles when needed to sustain our positions. While there wasn't much innovation and little of our marketing at the time truly changed behavior, we were capable, vastly profitable and it was a great community to be in.

It was a macro technology and connectivity trend that made the difference. The Internet was exploding. While many companies were in the early days of understanding its impact, innovative commerce platforms with new business models were beginning to spring up everywhere. I don't remember how many of our brands even had a website back then. Those that did mainly offered the nutritional information on the pack and some marketing copy to reward you for persevering through the pain of those glacially slow dial-up connections.

As the dotcom bubble grew, investors reappraised the CPG industry. They noticed that there wasn't a lot of growth by comparison. The capital flight and re-rating happened in a matter of weeks. As pressure mounted internally on growth, I found myself part of two simultaneous strategy initiatives.

The first exercise was exciting. It was to be the start of defining a new growth culture that would shift this behemoth into the rapidly approaching 21st century. This of course assumed no Y2K disasters, the preparations for which dominated the waking hours of about a third of the firm. Those meetings were to be avoided at all costs. The idea was to run a competition across the European region for new growth ideas. The winners would not only secure funding, they would also gain equity stakes in their idea. As this was mission critical, they would be immediately relieved of whatever operational duties they had and asked to focus on their new ideas with career guarantees that this would be a leapfrog not a sideshow.

As it transpired this was my first experience of an over-engineered, reassuringly expensive consulting project. I remember the briefing call where the lead consultant lambasted us with dotcom growth examples and asked why our margarine brands hadn't embraced the internet. Although my memory is hazy, I am confident there wasn't a single example from consumer goods. He then moved on to the competition requirements which amounted to "an idea". Not a validated idea or a business plan. Just an idea and the confidence that Unilever could fund whatever was necessary. What was critically important was to understand how the ideas would be evaluated. Here comes the 2x2 matrix!

The ideas would be looked at through two lenses. Whether the market existed or not, and whether it fit with Unilever's business model. The twist was that the winners would predominantly be selected from the "disruptive" space (new markets that had nothing to do with Unilever's business model). This avoided us coming up with safe ideas and instead we would champion ideas in markets that didn't exist, requiring capabilities we didn't have. In the interests of brevity, I will spare you the rest. A lot of money was spent. It didn't last. It didn't make a difference to growth.

Simultaneously, a big and expensive business strategy exercise was underway, using the Hax process. It was a great privilege to be involved, as this process carried kudos. It centered on exceptional amounts of market data translated into an inordinate number of market definitions (most of which were different to the way the consumer viewed the world). Then came an executive effort to word-smith the forms that laid out the critical logic linking mission to vision to strategy. What was a tactic and what was a strategic thrust? These were all being sent to the regional team, had we used the mandatory language in all the areas we were required to? Apparently, nomenclature could kill the best strategy if appropriate convention wasn't followed!

Similar to the first exercise, the conclusion from these vast paper-filled binders was the identification of market segments we didn't play in and a proposal for heavily funded entries into the same. On closer inspection there would be a codename for the project and a P&L loss estimate which seemed to budget little revenue and lots of investment. The only consumer data I could see in the whole process was usage and habits studies which invariably modeled accelerated decline of existing business and exponential growth in the categories the codename projects related to, even when these were mature markets.

I learned a lot from this time. At a macro level, how capricious Wall Street affection is for an industry, let alone a company. Within the business, it was fascinating to see how few ideas there were for the core. Our lifeblood was almost viscerally rejected as pressure hit. It didn't seem rational. There was an array of hard facts on competitive metrics to show how strong our business was, but those metrics didn't translate into the confidence to grow. This was a truly marketing-led company and the enormous marketing teams seemed to have much greater passion to be the brand they didn't own or in the market they didn't participate in. The core was simply a cash cow to fund high risk investments in new business that seemed to have little long-term potential to replicate the strength of the core. As my career progressed, I discovered that a lack of ideas to grow established brands was a common problem.

Of course, the dotcom bubble burst. Investors returned to consumer goods stocks which were rebranded as reliable, unlikely to lose your money and, better still, had huge margin opportunities ahead. The obsession with growth quietly waned. A 20-year bull-run of savings opportunities took its place. Outsourcing, offshoring, overhead reduction, and business services projects moving IT to outside providers. Simplification was highly prized as a route to more coherent and focused portfolios and cheaper organizations. The lingering emphasis on growth became about portfolio momentum. This was the era of BRIC, then BRICMIST, then BRIC +100m population markets. Companies sought growth through market momentum by repositioning to faster growing geographies. They used M&A to change the weight of category mix, selling the laggards and buying growth.

These were not trivial times in our industry. In the 80s and 90s, there was a great diversity within the CPG giants. A rational process of industry focus was followed by category focus and then brand focus. This led to large disposals, portfolio re-shaping and a heightened focus on acquisitions to replenish the loss of scale and spend surplus financial capacity. Capital was plowed into venture units for investment in early stage businesses. Combined with outsourcing a lot of production, we saw a seismic shift in value from assets and manufacturing to brands and goodwill. 84% of company value is now in intangibles, up from 32% in 1985.[1]

20 YEARS OF BENCHMARKING AND INCREASINGLY BLOATED BALANCE SHEETS

The last 20 years has been the era of the benchmark and the balance sheet. The cost work came first. Ruthless peer comparisons were made on every ratio. Zero based budgeting systematically picked up every rock to find hidden indulgences and stamp on them. Billions of dollars were plowed into annual restructuring programs. Partners in consumer research, advertising and creative saw budgets continuously reduced. New budgeting frameworks developed – remember HOG, ZOG, NOG? This cost work was so powerful it got the industry through the great recession with significant earnings growth intact. The financial crisis unlocked the balance sheet accelerator. A new era of unprecedented and sustained cheap money. Real interest rates for even the weakest businesses were near to zero and the appetite for leverage was enabled by a near limitless level of liquidity. Organic earnings growth was driven by savings programs and inorganic returns were fueled by leveraged acquisitions and share buy backs. Growth came and went. It was certainly rewarded when sustained, but it wasn't overly punished when weak. Savings and balance sheets could create more than adequate value. Geographic expansion didn't survive the threat it posed to margin and the bumps of various economic crises. Investors generally favored faster and more certain paths to value. That same debate will soon return for many companies.

These benchmark and balance sheet dynamics feasted on each other and created incredible returns for even average businesses. Maintenance strategies could suddenly be value creating and didn't need bold moves for breakout levels of performance. In fact, those strategies were risky relative to the "cash cow + credit" approach.

WE ARE NOW FACING THE CONSEQUENCES OF 20 YEARS OF BENCHMARKING AND BORROWING.

New perceived wisdoms grew up that were counter-intuitive. High levels of debt seemed value creating and low risk, while low levels of debt were "uneconomic." Owning assets was deemed "inefficient," despite the low cost of capital. Sale and leasebacks were more "value creating," despite the margin lost and the ultra-long-term commitments made. Share buy-backs went from stigma to standard. Handing back significant capital to investors used to mean you had run out of ideas to create value from your business and was frowned upon. Now it became a badge of honor for shareholder friendliness. Meanwhile, large holding companies could sustain significantly higher multiples than those attributed to the brands they were acquiring. The sum of the parts bore little relation to … the sum of the parts.

Perhaps most important was the notion that this model was enduring, not temporary. Surely it could go on forever? Surely it had no limits? Margins had no ceiling, and cost levels had no floor. Working capital could be negative. EBITDA could only ever rise, so leverage ratios must inevitably go down, fueling future borrowing capacity. Top line growth wasn't necessary to create value or to future proof a business against marketplace changes. The world would never change. Which meant that growth investments and innovation could be cut.

GROWTH IS THE ACID TEST OF RELEVANCE WITH CONSUMERS AND CUSTOMERS.

That's how we got to where we are. A 20-year low on organic sales growth, and an unprecedented cumulative high on leverage, share repurchases and restructuring programs. We don't have much growth because we didn't need it to create value. Looking ahead, growth is likely to be the most impactful lever. In a fast-changing world, growth will be the acid test of sustained and increased relevance to customers and consumers. This will not be as simple as turning on a tap. Many of the cost saving choices were made without concern for growth capabilities which are now weakened just when we need them most. Large firms created space for insurgents by delisting lower priority brands in pursuit of complexity reduction. Short-term sales focus has increased, and so short-term levers are pulled more frequently and more firmly.

In many categories, innovation is greater from small brands than larger brands. The big budget household names often focus on low increment derivative activity relying on promotions to drive sales.

"Capabilities for growth are weakened just when we need them most."

Within marketing departments there are lower investments in training and reluctance to invest in consumer understanding. Equally, there is less appreciation of specialization in research and marketing with a focus on generalists as a route to savings.

This is the backdrop and context to the situation we face today. The first growth crisis was really one of comparison – industries came and went in Wall Street enthusiasm. Many dotcom businesses weren't sustainable. What followed was a logical, safe and highly valuable set of interventions in the basic wiring of the consumer products industry. 20 years of resetting the value chain. A transformation in how and where products are made and how back office functions are managed. A permanent step-change in the acceptable level of overhead to run a business and the cost to support brands. A great deal of value was created, enhanced by more aggressive use of balance sheets to increase shareholder returns. This next growth crisis has the potential to reshape the industry. Markets are fundamentally changing. We are seeing heightened competition between insurgent and mature brands. We are seeing substantial disruption in channels as online growth accelerates and brick & mortar struggles to adapt quickly enough. Meanwhile, technology and digital continue as accelerants of change, escalating in impact as scale and adoption rises. We are several years into this new challenge already, but so far impact and response have been incremental. We don't enter this new phase in good shape. Organic growth for CPG companies in the developed world is close to zero. The levers of the last 20 years are waning – balance sheets are levered, cost programs are reducing in scale of impact, assets have already been sold.

This period will polarize winners and losers. Facing disruption is a tough place to be. Decisions are difficult and there are no easy answers with so many stakeholders and trade-offs. Employees, communities, shareholders, bond holders, suppliers, unions, and many more. Change will be necessary, speed and flexibility essential. External focus and impact with consumers and customers will make the difference to value creation. Long-term sustainable growth can only be achieved if organizations take the time and effort to create their own solutions to their own unique set of challenges. They will need to look deep into their own organizations. That's where the well-spring of solutions already exist. It will be a time to navigate uncertainty with optimism, bring clarity to complex situations and a common understanding to all stakeholders.

What created value in the past two decades will not be enough to win in the 2020s. The drivers of change are converging and accelerating. Conditions that created stability for the past 30 years are unravelling. Markets will look very different in 10-20 years. Consumer and shopper behaviors are evolving with substantial change in the retail footprint. Use growth strategy to force your organization to embrace the required change to be future ready. There is much to consider, much to do and no time to waste.

THE WORLD IS CHANGING.

GROWTH FORCES US TO CHANGE WITH IT.

THE BEST WILL CHANGE AHEAD OF IT.

CHAPTER THREE

THE PIVOT POINT

The last 20 years saw unprecedented intervention in the value chain of the CPG industry. This was not a minor procedure. It was major surgery. Cost levels fundamentally changed. We reset the basic parameters of what was owned, what was on-shore and what was done in-house.

The playbook created incredible value, despite the challenges of the Global Financial Crisis and the distraction of more than a decade of business re-engineering. How was it possible that so many companies could focus inwardly for so long on the redesign of their core operations? The answer is fairly simple. Stability came from commonality of strategy across the industry and from entrenched market structures.

Almost every company was following the same playbook, allowing partners and suppliers to scale up. Great learning effects were achieved across the industry because most companies were working on the same things at the same time. Capabilities built by the larger firms with bigger budgets trickled down to smaller companies. This was serious business. Consulting and outsourcing companies saw prodigious expansion. Progress accelerated with the evolution of more flexible and more remote technology.

At the same time, in most product categories the market structure was firmly entrenched. The top 3-4 suppliers and a handful of customers dominated market share (typically 70%+). This was the external stability that enabled internal transformation and protected profit pools. While there were always micro-battles, at macro level, profits shifted only incrementally between major players. Suppliers enjoyed 3-4x the margins of retailers with much less fixed cost. Bumps in the road could normally be smoothed out with balance sheet capacity and pricing for inflation. Even the Global Financial Crisis did little more to CPG than temporarily reduce the rate of earnings growth.

I have spent a lot of time on trends through my strategy career. It is difficult to make trend work actionable and impactful enough to be the foundation of strategy. These are insights that few people want to pay for, and so outside solutions are often generic. I have learned that to do trend work well requires a blend of skills in analytics, consumer understanding, futuring and visualization. Change tends to happen slowly until trends intersect, and impact accelerates. We're seeing this effect now in consumer goods. Trends in consumer habits, channel rotation and technology are converging. Add to this the multi-year fallout from COVID-19, and you have a perfect storm.

THE FORCES OF STABILITY ARE GIVING WAY TO THE FORCES OF CHANGE.

Not everyone has understood the magnitude of shift that is taking place. Boardrooms are filled with leaders in their 50s and 60s who have grown up in an industry defined by stability. They made the "cash cow + credit" model work extremely well through their careers. They see the future as the same as the past. They have similar backgrounds and a common perspective. Long tenures, which are all too common, breed incrementalism and institutionalized thinking. A perception of boardroom ineffectiveness and lack of diversity of opinion are some of the main drivers of activism.

A recent Harvard article determined 93% of executives are grappling with volatility in their markets with 68% saying they don't understand the best way forward to achieve agility and innovation. Half of those surveyed believe the biggest challenge is reconciling transformation efforts to the existing business model.[1]

INCREMENTAL THINKING IS INADEQUATE AND GREAT ARE THE PERILS OF INACTION.

The next era will be defined by change and change management. Lasting change is built on deliberate strategy. There are real pressures on organizations, pressures that present both existential threats and profound opportunity. AI, automation, technological advancement, 3-D printing, demographic changes, climate change, let alone societal issues such as increased populism and income inequality. This creates a VUCA environment. Capacity to change will be central to future competitive advantage.

The winners will be those who can conceive a new future and rapidly re-position their business to take advantage of it. The opportunities will be vast and fast. In contrast, cash cow strategies will no longer be viable because industry profit pools are finally shifting. Diseconomies of scale are appearing for firms that built themselves around limiting change to maximize profitability. The words of the famous disclaimer, "past performance is not an indicator of future results," have never been more true. Scale that was seen as a blessing for profitability can be a curse when it comes to making rapid change. While firms work to tackle new challenges, consumers can change behavior immediately and with no nostalgia or sympathy for companies that can't keep up.

For much of the last 20 years there was abundant opportunity to increase profitability across the value chain. Today there is much less juice left to squeeze. At the same time many balance sheets are now substantially levered and so organic performance will be more important to results. This is where the market dynamics converge to challenge the balance and strength of our plans. There are pressures mounting throughout the typical P&L.

Customer profitability is hard to optimize when winners and losers are polarizing. The customers you want to pull money from are often high margin and in danger of going out of business. They'll make dramatic decisions and create risk for your base business. The winners are winning big and they want to be paid accordingly. It's expensive to win in an omni-channel environment and leading retailers need money to invest as well as earnings growth to reward their shareholders. Price transparency caps the potential to charge more to protect margins. Meanwhile, many retailers follow a value proposition driving down prices wherever possible. Other growth channels like Club and Off-Price are low margin at the best of times, deliberately brand agnostic to drive negotiating leverage.

THE BATTLE OF THE BRANDS BETWEEN INSURGENTS AND HOUSEHOLD NAMES

It is equally hard for big brands to pull back on promotions when there are over 10,000 insurgent brands fighting at lower margins. Innovation that grows the category is a good answer, but the metrics say this is in short supply. It's been replaced by an abundance of lower impact derivative activity that is faster and cheaper to develop. Scale is an albatross in a dynamic marketplace unless scale can be converted into advantage through bigger impact or bolder decision making. Short-term results pressure often leads larger brands to neglect this critical advantage and "act small".

In the supply chain, many companies now self-manufacture less than half of their products. A large number of brands, especially insurgents, have no factories. Most sourcing is done on a multi-national basis. Businesses have worked on these levers for nearly 30 years. The major shifts to make or buy, source cross-border, squeeze suppliers, automate and re-engineer have all been taken.

Commitments to sustainability will drive greater material complexity, trial of smaller quantities and less proven supply routes. All of which will reverse some of the margin gains businesses have achieved. There is no evidence the consumer will pay more for this and it is therefore likely to be many years before sustainable supply chains can recreate the economics of legacy. An industry-wide approach will foster innovation and speed progress towards solutions and better economics.

Another dis-synergy may come from the big brands increasing their response to insurgents. Homogeneity of format has created innovation space on simple dimensions like pack form, pack size and product design. Cutting the brand tail improved supply chain complexities for large firms but leaves them with an inadequate portfolio to cover all consumer needs and a leaky bucket of operating income. Some of these decisions will likely be revisited, and portfolio management skills will become an essential part of marketing again. Where online sales are significant, brands fight for awareness, trial and repeat in highly complex marketplaces with infinite aisles and always-on digital demand creation. Many marketing models were built for the finite shelf and controllable media universes of the past. While the challenge of cut-through favors scale, the pace of change favors insurgents unburdened by legacy. The stage is set for the battle of the brands, each with strengths and weaknesses in their business model. The challenges of scale set against the challenges of scaling. Insurgents have not yet faced a full-tilt big-brand fightback and many new brands come and go. The early sales to establish a franchise are much easier than the ideas and investment needed to scale to critical mass.

For many companies, there is far less opportunity to reduce overhead costs than there used to be after a decade or more of frequent restructuring. Cost cutting and "same for less" thinking has been the more common approach, rather than re-engineering to generate true efficiencies. Many brand budgets are lower in consumer research and, in some cases, advertising. Marketing organizations are much smaller than 10-15 years ago. At the same time, there's significant inflation on overheads in rising wages, healthcare and pension costs. These pressures make it even more difficult to fund investments for growth.

Against this challenging backdrop, investor guidance limits degrees of freedom. Margin targets require continuous improvement after inflationary effects are offset. Earnings are typically expected to increase by at least upper single digits. Share repurchases have been profound drivers of EPS with many companies lowering share counts significantly. Balance sheet capacity is reducing and post COVID-19 there may well be less acceptance of these mechanics, especially when funded by debt. Acquiring EPS by accretive deals is becoming more difficult with deal multiples averaging 3-5 turns above where they were a decade ago and with synergies waning after all the cost work already done in target companies.

The pressure of the pivot is upon us. 50% of CEOs believe their investors only look at short-term metrics.[2] C-Suite turnover is increasing dramatically. 2019 saw a 40% spike in CEO departures from the 10-year trend.[3] External replacements doubled, becoming the majority for the first time in years. Of all industries, CPG saw the highest rate of departures, with nearly 200 CEOs leaving. CMO tenure is now down to little more than two years, an impossible time period to materially influence marketing strategy and innovation.[4]

"Turnover in the c-suite is rising with mounting pressure."

There are additional challenges in ownership structures. The first is Private Equity, which currently has an incredible amount of investment dry powder. They historically allocated around 15% of investment to CPG.[5] Private Equity is building a new model of value creation after "strip it and flip it" expired. Target acquisitions are too expensive and have had too much cost work done already to make that model adequate for the price paid. To create value, and to be confident on exit strategy, Private Equity will need to adapt to prioritizing business development. They may also develop far greater platform thinking, applying a longer-term perspective and bundling synergistic assets together. Platforms can unlock cost and revenue synergies, diversify risk and give scale that increases exit options.

In a Private Equity model, the challenge for companies is the ownership time horizon. This is now less than 5 years on average.

So, the pressure ramps. The brief to management is a full cycle of designing, developing and delivering a new path to value creation within this compressed ownership period. While this has been accomplished many times before, this was in more stable markets. Today's volatile market conditions will affect the certainty of success. The temptation historically to focus on turnarounds and lower multiple acquisitions is now less wise. Distinguishing turnaround potential from terminal decline will be a difficult judgment. At the same time, high debt levels can create inflexible business models that reduce a company's ability to change and fuel the risk of value destruction. The playbook will need to evolve if the available cash is to be put to work well.

The second ownership dynamic is shareholder activism. There are nearly 1,000 campaigns a year across industries, up from only a handful a decade ago. Around 250 board seats are won a year through campaigns, almost all in negotiated settlement. CPG however, accounts for only 7% of total campaigns, despite 30% of surveyed analysts highlighting the industry as a top target for activism. About a quarter of campaigns are on outperforming stocks and so this is an issue that affects even high performers. Only 4% of campaigns are about organic business strategy. M&A and governance dominate.[6] The fear of activism in the c-suite is likely to be a magnitude higher than these statistics show. Increasingly everyone knows someone who has been involved in a campaign, and this is becoming major business for the investment banks.

Pressure is mounting. Pressure from all sides. Our well-worn safety blankets are largely worn out. The outlook is stormy. In tough conditions, it is the strongest who survive. The question for all leaders now is whether you can make opportunity from change. Put simply, is this your pivot point or your breaking point? Maintenance leaders will not cut it. Cash cow strategy will no longer be adequate. We lost momentum on growth because we didn't need it to achieve our financial objectives. We need it now more than ever. We need it for earnings. We need it to galvanize the future focus and change required. We need it to convey confidence in our ability to stay relevant to our customers and consumers.

"I NEVER WORRY ABOUT ACTION, BUT ONLY INACTION."

-WINSTON CHURCHILL

CHAPTER FOUR

LETTING GO OF LEGACY

I worked for Paul Polman as head of strategy at Unilever for the first 3 years of his tenure. He was the only outside CEO in the company's history. An inspiring leader whom I learned a great deal from. His most frequent quote in speeches was an adaptation of the racing car driver Mario Andretti, "When things around me are moving faster than I am, I know I'm I trouble." It was Paul's way of saying we are in a VUCA world but what matters is how well we respond. That's how we win. It's a lesson that stuck with me.

It's tough for organizations to know how best to respond to a fast-changing world. Instinctively, they know that what got them to where they are may not be enough to get them to where they need to go. The reality is that decades of legacy thinking can be stifling, but removing it all too quickly can leave people feeling lost and vulnerable. It's like removing a well-worn safety blanket. When organizations start to radically reshape strategy and systems, they often don't pay enough attention to changing mindsets and behaviors. It's a bit like changing the hardware but keeping the old software. What's needed is a proper upgrade.

As an industry, we have some groupthink to leave behind. It will not all be easy to let go of, and it is not always clear what comes next. That's why culture and change management are as much a part of strategy as the bold ideas and concepts. What will it mean to pivot our thinking to creating opportunity from change? Embracing a future that may be significantly different from the past. Innovation, fresh thinking and agility are needed. We must make strides forward, not small steps. Managing legacy must give way to pursuing progress. Future potential will increasingly drive current performance.

WE'RE ALL INDIVIDUALS

For the last 20 years, the value creation playbook across most consumer product companies has been incredibly homogeneous. While the starting points were different, the formula for success was consistent:

LOW VOLUME GROWTH + COMMODITY INFLATION PRICING = LOW SALES GROWTH

OUTSOURCE, OFFSHORE, SIMPLIFY, CUT = HIGH PROFIT GROWTH

HIGH PROFIT GROWTH + RETURN OF CASH TO SHAREHOLDERS = VERY HIGH TSR

ENHANCE BY SELLING LOW GROWTH + BUYING HIGH SYNERGY OR HIGH GROWTH

You can't deny it worked consistently well, while it worked. As time goes on and the world changes, the hidden costs that never made the business case will become clear. Building back advantage will be hard.

As a Brit with a sarcastic sense of humor, I couldn't resist offering the scene in Monty Python's *Life of Brian* where hundreds chant in unison, "we're all individuals!" Google it; it'll do it more justice than I can begin to.

This was the era of benchmarking. The dominant logic of the whole value chain was to work with large consulting firms designing how to be the same as everyone else. The triumph of homogeneity! It did lasting damage to the consumer offer. Research budgets were cut. Products, packaging and brands were harmonized for remorseless efficiency. Formulations weakened and packs shrank to mask price increases. No one imagined insurgent brands could fill the vacuum and come for lunch. We thought consumers and customers would simply take what they were given.

Benchmarking was about maximizing profits, ultimately at the expense of the consumer. Now the world has changed, and many businesses have no real response. They designed themselves for a different world. Making money meant sacrificing flexibility. Differentiation was expensive. Change was inefficient. Real strategy is about competitive advantage. Real marketing is about your USP. How did we lose sight of this? The hidden costs are coming to the fore. Innovation is a necessity not an indulgence. We must all be individuals again, plotting our own path, putting customers and consumers first.

LETTING GO OF LEGACY

NOT YOUR GRANDMA'S

Most companies talk about innovation, but how much do we really deliver? If we judge ourselves against the Founders that created the brands and categories we now operate, what have we actually built that's new?

Before you answer, ask yourself, for any given product you use as a consumer, how does today's latest and greatest compare to what your grandparents used? Is it really different? I would argue that our kitchens, closets, bathrooms and pantries are all stuffed with more expensive versions of the same things that have existed for generations. Has the razor fundamentally changed? Has soap? Has Mac & Cheese? No! The experiences may be bigger, better and certainly more expensive, but are they fundamentally different? If not, what level of innovation should we be able to deliver?

I spent 14 years at Unilever. This was a business built on nearly 100 years of category creation. Unilever had a mission and a repeatable model that was as profound in its impact on society as it was in building an enormous conglomerate.

Unilever took unique insights and created meaningful benefits in new products that were accessible – through affordability, wide distribution and mass-marketing. It was a multi-local business strategy. The ideas were routinely adapted to local living standards and the most impactful distribution and advertising models in any country. Management was predominantly indigenous to ensure the effective and efficient local translation of the global concept. The business was designed around everyday needs and accessibility to consumers, creating large markets. Margarine for health, soap and detergents for hygiene, Dove for self-esteem and Axe the mating game for emotional beauty. All accessible, all available, all widely relevant.

This was a truly innovative business model spanning generations. Doing well by doing good. Category creation. Scalable ideas. Turning insight into action. Purpose powering profit. Repeatability.

The standards of our Founders are the standards we should all live by. We should be aspirational. We should set big goals and not be satisfied with tactical activity. Variants and incrementalism have their place in commercial plans, but let's not kid ourselves. In a fast-changing world real innovation is the benchmark. Go create something new and find your way to scale it. You have exponentially more resources than your Founders did. Put them to work, purposefully and persistently.

LETTING GO OF LEGACY

THE CURSE OF INCREMENTALISM

There is a hard fact in life. What got you to where you are today is predominantly a sunk cost. It's hard to accept after all the effort, but what matters is what happens next.

When planning the future, time is a crucial variable because degrees of freedom go up exponentially with time. Yet so many individuals and businesses focus only on what's next in the sense of tomorrow versus today. They spend much less time thinking about next year, let alone the next decade. Their measure of progress is an abundance of immediate problem solving, rather than the application of imagination and energy to the longer-term. This is the triumph of the maintenance team over the architects. Fix a leak, save money, and everyone will be happy. Nothing gets built, no new horizons are tested. This is the curse of incrementalism.

A Nasdaq study sent to the SEC in 2019 cataloged the short-termism across corporate America. 74% of respondents said that nearly half their investors valued short-term returns over long-term and a similar number felt pressured not to make long-term investments. The same executives reported that less than 40% of Boards considered a time horizon of 3 years or more.[1]

To break the cycle, we need to start at the end. If you start with where you are today and try to work out what's currently wrong, and what needs fixing, you'll simply project forward your problems, and your solutions will be quick fixes. If on the other hand you start at the end and look backwards, it's easier to see that what got you to the starting point is not going to get you to your new objective. Legacy systems and processes, legacy thinking and legacy people may all need to change.

The answers lie within, but you have to create the right conditions to find them. Starting at the end and looking back provides a totally different perspective. Cast off the shackles of incrementalism and change will flow, further and faster, from within your own organization.

LETTING GO OF LEGACY

THE HUNGER GAMES

The battle ground is set between big brands and their insurgent challengers. The question for many insurgents is how to determine their full potential and develop enough scale to create a sustainable model. For the big brands the question is how to leverage scale advantage and better portfolio strategy to cover more consumer space and develop the high impact ideas that build categories.

There have always been well-understood unmet needs and niche preference drivers in every category. The big brands had to be selective because shelf space was finite. They prioritized the primary drivers of preference and the priority unmet needs for innovation. They picked the best technology and benefits to deliver performance on the attributes that mattered most. There have always been alternative formulations but they were usually less effective. The big brands left a lot on the table – maybe 10-15%

of a category – and they knew it. In the old world, it wasn't cost effective to pursue. Many smaller brands with well established equity were delisted in favor of supply chain efficiencies. This created portfolio gaps and the space for new entrants.

The battle of the brands is a story of lower barriers to entry. Historically, the barriers were the concentration of share in the big brands and big customers, entrenched by the high cost and zero-sum game of mass media. eCommerce and digital marketing have quickly dismantled this with infinite aisles and always-on digital demand creation. New brands have arrived, in the thousands. While consumer habits may not have changed much, the proliferation of choice has fueled niches, personalization and design expectations that big homogeneous brands have failed to satisfy.

Yet markets don't change as quickly as people would have you believe. Preference drivers in well-defined and well-established categories move very slowly. Do not let turf wars over the tertiary unmet needs blindside you to this. If they do move, it takes a great deal of marketing investment, a major event like regulation, or a technical breakthrough. Every digital brand with a hyper growth rate on a small base will try to convince you otherwise. Rationally follow the consumer.

The battle has challenges for both David and Goliath. If you are a big brand, should you have left so much open space now that there are well-established and economic routes to fill out your brand? If you are an insurgent brand, torture your potential and obsess about what you can do better than the big brands on a sustainable basis. Spend big once you have that edge. Until you do, don't believe your own b.s. and early phase sales.

LETTING GO OF LEGACY

CHANGE YOUR CHANGE MANAGEMENT

For decades the practices of Kaizen, 5S, 6S, Lean and continuous improvement have pervaded all competent manufacturing facilities. Quality and safety are a given, always measured and never sacrificed. Automation is an opportunity to apply human capital to higher order tasks and robotics to the menial. There is a constant mission to lower costs and lead-times by doing things better. It's achieved by reimagination, not simply by cutting. Designs come from the people that know best on the ground, not from 30,000 feet. No matter how many times a process has been improved, there's always a belief that more can be done. That is why we all love visiting well-run plants – there are few more satisfying sights than watching value creation happen in real time.

Contrast this now with the change programs you find in overheads. Change is almost always a euphemism for cuts. Cutting is not about efficiency. Cutting leaves the same work in the hands of fewer people. Productivity doesn't go up because you create increased levels of stress. All the real work still needs to be done. Cuts are measured incrementally (and often optimistically) and so each individual change seems rational. Over a period of time the capabilities of a business are fundamentally altered and become more limited. The opportunity cost is never in the business case.

There is a universal truth that costs are a one-way street. Whether we have cut too far or not, costs are not getting added back. So, to fund new growth strategies and new capabilities we have to learn to create genuine efficiencies. Strategy can guide this. In defining what matters most, you automatically define what matters less. Fragmentation of tactics is a great source of waste in many business plans. Subscale activity can be little better than no activity. By saving a bit, you can waste a lot. Inconsistency is a root cause of inefficiency. Consistent direction, clear prioritization and measurable activity-based execution. These are the foundations on which efficiencies can be built.

It's perfectly reasonable to expect better. Look at the behaviors and attitudes needed to succeed in the new environment. Collaboration, curiosity, the ability to work in self-created, self-governing teams with cross-functional mindsets. Sounds a lot like those Kaizen teams that have operated for decades in your factories. It's time to step it up at HQ.

MANAGE WHAT YOU MEASURE

Rewarding and recognizing the right behaviors instills change in your organization and inspires your best people to give their best. How you look at this topic transforms how you view the world. Companies have a bias to measure the things that are easy to measure and use these metrics for targets, budgets and incentives.

Before you can decide on your metrics, you must be clear about your strategy. What matters most and what most needs to change. It is natural to begin measuring new things when you have a new strategy. If nothing changes in your assessment of outcomes, it is likely nothing is changing in your inputs. So, a critical step to embedding strategy is to be clear on what needs to be different, in direction, order of magnitude and time horizon.

The biggest impediment is a lack of clear delineation of inputs, outputs and outcomes. The people dimension and the metrics side of it are almost inseparable. Your culture is defined by behaviors and ways of working. People and metrics are a huge part of that. The strategist designs towards outcomes, which in turn are rigorously measured and ruthlessly prioritized. The imperative is to recognize and reward the people and behaviors that deliver outcomes. This breathes life and longevity into the strategy.

Inputs are the most basic element of business. In behavior terms, these are the doers. People who are constantly busy, walking purposefully, always in meetings and on the phone, on email 24/7, and traveling constantly. This is behavior that often gets noticed. A badge of honor of commitment. It's also a symbol of churn – the triumph of the urgent over the important.

Outputs are what make people stand out. These are the campaigners who deliver the goods. Launching products, building factories and making advertising. These leaders are important, but they rely on established process to make progress.

Outcomes are the most difficult. This is where people start at the end and work backwards. They focus on real change. Change in habits, behaviors, purchasing decisions, reputations. They focus on making new things happen. These are the achievers.

Transformation cannot be achieved by simply adding up a set of inputs, many of which will be legacy based. Transformation flows from a point of view on the future and the repositioning of your business to win. Start with the end in mind. Create the necessary conditions of consistency, commitment and reward to let the achievers make things happen.

LETTING GO OF LEGACY

A CONSTRUCTIVE CULTURE

I object to the idea that execution is strategy. The reason for this is simple. Every business needs a point of view on the future. A business that isn't progressing is actually regressing because the world is moving against you. You will see in this book many of the ways in which the world is changing rapidly. The drivers of this change are already 10-20 years in the making, so impact is accelerating. The maintenance teams running cash cow strategies and optimizing short-term financials are about to get their bluffs called. It isn't less risky to be a cash cow, it's now more risky.

Balance sheets made average organic performers look outstanding in the last decade. For a while, it was possible to optimize short-term earnings by avoiding long-term challenges and focusing on quick wins. Teams that were increasing promotions and cutting long-term investments weren't creating real value, they were running a business down. Slowly but surely. Teams that have been built to pull these levers will not know how to pivot in this environment. Instead they will cling on too long to declining customers, legacy relationships, legacy product. They will be afraid to pursue eCommerce in case it is less profitable, even as their competitors do. They'll use short-term P&L scenarios that say earnings will be greater this year and next if we do it all the old way. A new way is too risky.

We need to institutionalize leadership that values building things. Leaders with vision who can translate vision to reality – building new products, new categories, new geographies and new capabilities. Sometimes from scratch, sometimes not. Leaders who can breathe life into mature situations and move them back on trend. Leaders who see growth and efficiencies from embracing technology. Leaders who recognize that the future will be different from the past, both in the core business model and footprint. Leaders who can smartly sequence change and reallocate resources to build big while making the numbers work. Leaders who can experiment with an eye to scalability. Leaders who create a culture of change and doing new things.

This is the age of building. Future value and future proofing are inextricably linked. The winners will win big. There is much opportunity in change. If you want to be a winner you can't stand still, you've gotta get moving.

" IMPOSSIBLE IS JUST A BIG WORD THROWN AROUND BY SMALL MEN WHO FIND IT EASIER TO LIVE IN THE WORLD THEY'VE BEEN GIVEN THAN TO EXPLORE THE POWER THEY HAVE TO CHANGE IT.

IMPOSSIBLE IS NOT A FACT,
IT'S AN OPINION.

IMPOSSIBLE IS NOT A DECLARATION,
IT'S A DARE.

IMPOSSIBLE IS POTENTIAL.

IMPOSSIBLE IS TEMPORARY.

IMPOSSIBLE" IS NOTHING.

–MUHAMMAD ALI

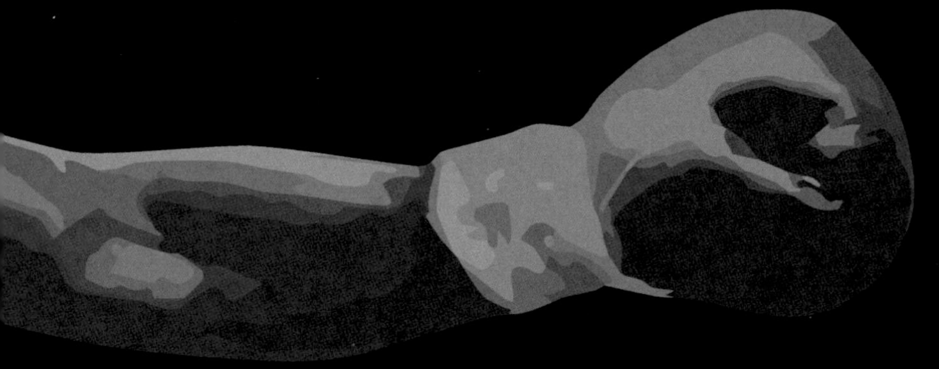

CHAPTER FIVE

THE POWER OF BUILDING SOMETHING

I realized in writing this book that two of my greatest orthodoxies have been in happy but silent conflict for years. I have always been an advocate of the school of thought that, "what got you here won't get you there." Tacit complacency and inaction are two of the greatest risks facing brands and business teams. It seems to me that much of the role of the strategist is to future proof an organization by helping teams prepare for and then create a different future. At the same time, I have found the past and future are inextricably linked. The first thing I do when looking to understand any new business is to learn the Founder's story and, more importantly, the story behind it. The history usually holds some of the solution and much of the inspiration for the future.

The back story has deep meaning. You find the purpose of the original idea that created the brand or the business we know today. The reason to be. The insight that delivered a new product and a consumer experience good enough to change behavior. Marketing strategy 101, but more than that. People join industries like consumer goods and healthcare because of the potential to make a difference in people's lives. The people who create brands often risk everything because they can't live with an under-served market. Founders bring meaning to marketing. They create ideas that change a market, and often with a fraction of the resources and knowledge that established businesses have. They do it because they care deeply enough to act. They do it because they have to.

Lessons from Founders serve us well. When I was President of a Fortune 500 company, I had a pack of cards made with a card for each of the top 52 brands. Each card had the Founder, launch date and an image of the first product ever made. It was a daily inspiration on my desk. I learned many things from the Founders I worked with, but one thread stands out. The combination of great clarity of purpose with consistency of execution delivers exponential growth in the team and in the business. What was striking was the comparison of progress in Founder models with traditional corporate experiences. It was night and day. The corporate model seemed designed not to change. It focused on learning to do the same things over and over again rather than doing anything new. The willingness to change and the pace of change were profoundly different as a result.

I first realized the power of consistency from Sami El-Saden, the Founder of Contigo, a reusable coffee mug and water bottle company. Sami started his career in big business. With a passion for technology and innovation, he decided to go in a more entrepreneurial direction. He worked with me for a long time after the Contigo acquisition, which was a commitment I truly appreciated. I got to know him well. His story of building the business had all the stops, starts, challenges and breakthroughs of any Founder story. What made the business successful and created a new category ahead of its time was Sami's consistent and laser focus on a simple but compelling business model.

Sami lived and breathed product. He built a partnership with a very capable supplier and built his firm internally around a Design culture. They obsessed about the technology needed to deliver a convenient on-the-go beverage product, adding spill-proof and leak-proof features to the industry standard insulation benefits. This was complimented with great form, feel and finish but it was the technology that made his brand stand apart. He worked tirelessly on that point of difference and recruited customer partners, creating the category for multiple retailers well before concerns about disposable beverage containers became mainstream. Sami never deviated from the mission but worked incredibly flexibly with his supplier and key customers to ensure the whole value chain worked. He listened to what both stakeholders needed to make a fast-growing business successful. He partnered rather than directed. His motivation was seeing his idea come to life, not any specific project details. Tactics would adapt to make the ideas more successful with his stakeholders, but the core mission of the business never wavered. This purpose pervaded the culture of the organization. Partnerships made the idea flourish.

This consistency and longevity is critical to the way that Founders distinguish themselves from most corporate leaders. Consistency applied to clarity of purpose has a multiplier effect across the team. Most business leaders I know have one or two businesses they truly admire. They can usually tell you why in a soundbite or two. If you then ask them to think about how that story was written, it dawns on them how long it took and how perseverance and purpose weathered all storms.

One of the major obstacles to successful strategy in corporations is consistency and tenure. Leaders want the next job as soon as they get the current job. They want to move up the ladder ahead of their peers. Internal promotion benchmarks are often what matters most. Performance is judged in a snapshot at the annual review. It is easy to optimize results for a known point in time. Today's tactics for today's results get rewarded, rather than the development of tomorrow's opportunities. Founders by contrast

"IF YOU REALLY LOOK CLOSELY, MOST OVERNIGHT SUCCESSES TOOK A LONG TIME."

-STEVE JOBS

are always judged on the historical trend in the context of the future opportunity. It's a fundamentally different way of assessing value and performance. The purpose driving the Founder defines the ambition and opportunity; the trend and track record defines progress. Founders need to show both to their investors if they are to scale their dreams. We remember the successful outcomes in valuation headlines, but the story is the journey. The journey is all about the growth of the business and the team.

Here in a nutshell is why my two orthodoxies were in conflict. I had one idea based on many years confronting unspoken inertia in corporations, and another learned from purpose driven Founders. Two angles on the same dynamic – the need to build to achieve true success and the multiplier effect that clarity and consistency brings in building something. Short-termism was not a deliberate intent in corporations, it was the inevitable consequence of inconsistency. Ideas were not pursued long enough to succeed. When pressures hit, the bolder ideas were the first to be abandoned in favor of tactical responses. It was a fool's paradise that favored the familiar and easier paths to short-term outcome over the challenge of building something new and sticking to it through thick and thin. Building something requires a Founder's attitude. It needs time and consistency of purpose to combine and create the multiplier effect. Creating the right conditions for success is as important to the strategy as the quality of ideas.

I learned how much growth can be achieved with consistency of mission from another Founder. One of the stories that has inspired me most in recent years is Brendan Lindsay, the Founder of Sistema plastics. He created a high growth business with incredible margins in a set of categories that, according to established wisdom, were commoditized. He started in New Zealand with plastic coat-hangers and ended up with a global brand presence in food, beverage and storage solutions. There were many things I learned from Brendan, but the story that most inspired me was the manufacturing side of the business. Sistema is proudly manufactured in Auckland in a modern, purpose built, state of the art facility. The factory and warehouse were designed after visiting the manufacturing and distribution centers of world-class companies. The team had built decades of knowledge in their own business but went to the next level by learning from the best in various industries and then trying to do it even better back home in New Zealand.

PURPOSE CREATES THE PLATFORM FOR GROWTH; CONSISTENCY BRINGS THE MULTIPLIER EFFECT.

A neat story in itself, but the best bit I learned over dinner with Brendan one night in his favorite Auckland restaurant. He was holding court with a wealth of anecdotes and the funniest was probably the most profound. When he started the coat hanger business, he bought his first machine and had a small garage space for production. He thought he could just plug the machine in. He soon learned he would need to get it properly installed and powered and got someone to take care of that. With relish he then set the machine going and went to the pub with his mate. When he returned a few hours later he expected to see the wealth created in his absence. Instead he found a mess of molten plastic. He didn't know the machine needed to be bolted to the floor. It had moved across to the other side of the garage and the production was a write-off. Brendan told me the story for a laugh, but it had a deeper impact on me. Imagine going from a garage mess to a world-class purpose-built facility and being acquired by a global conglomerate. A formidable journey of constant learning and challenge. It made me appreciate how far that business and team had come.

A CULTURE OF CONSTANT LEARNING AND ADAPTATION BUILDS THE TEAM AND THE BUSINESS.

Brendan's management approach was self-taught and idiosyncratic, but it was based on making things happen. His favorite saying was "don't be a can't". He cannot abide defeatism or negativity. He had big ambitions, and he was happy to give his team all they needed to realize them. He learned he needed people good enough to disagree with him as the business scaled. He learned that attitude and application in his team could make up for their experience gaps as long as they shared his vision and passion and were prepared to learn on the job. He built a culture around progress, not just in the product itself, but in the way it was made and distributed. As the company got bigger, Brendan wanted the best and he would spend what was needed to get it. It was never about perfection, but it was about continuously embracing new and better ways. He helped his team and business grow by the way he managed them. He had an eye for great detail, but the details wouldn't stand in the way of the vision. His vision was always about the end outcome he wanted, and he would take leaps in that direction, rejecting incremental changes in favor of bigger moves. Politics had no place in his business. What was right for

Sistema was right for Brendan. This philosophy led him to build a greenfield manufacturing site when he realized his current facilities could only ever be incrementally improved. Brendan knew a set of small steps would be more work and less impact than a big leap. Opened by the Prime Minister, the new facility was a punctuation point in a career that started with that molten mess of plastic on the garage floor.

Developing teams is critical to almost every Founder's story. Whenever I acquired a company, there was always an uncomfortable moment in the deal when we tried to lock down the key employment agreements and recruit leaders to the new chapter. This was when Founders would reveal how they were distributing the deal proceeds. In every situation, the Founders were exceptionally generous to the people that had helped them on the journey. These were rarely contractual entitlements. They were thoughtful, deeply appreciative moments of how the value had been created and a desire for the team to do exceptionally well. For us as new owners, it often took compensation out of the equation on retention. It forced us to do what really mattered and show the team how they could continue to bring their passion to realize even greater potential on the brands we were buying.

Founders truly reward their teams. First with loyalty and consistent tenure, then patience in performance as the growth journey stretches individuals, then sharing the value created. There would be outrage in our corporate functions each time these payments were disclosed because the team members had "less experience" than ours and "they couldn't possibly be worth that." This missed the point entirely. I appreciated through these processes

“DON’T BE A CAN’T.”

-BRENDAN LINDSAY

how deep expectation and entitlement can be in corporate life. Corporations often label pay and incentives as "reward." In reality, they treat people the same as much as they can with modest or little differentiation. They do this because it is seen as fair. Perhaps also because it is easy. We have seen an era of consistently high rewards. The median bonus payout for organizations in recent years has been 120% of target.[1] These metrics often benefited significantly from inorganic value creation. The new challenge will be how to pivot quickly to creating the time, space and rewards for those who can build what is central to future value.

While much will be demanded of larger brands, to act more quickly and more impactfully, there are also challenges for insurgents. There are more than 10,000 insurgent brands in CPG categories, but the vast majority never get to a single point of market share. The difficulties of scaling organically are profound - which is why we should learn as much as we can from those who have done it. All too often we celebrate the temporary disruptors. Attention seekers. Often with formidable consumer benefits but unsustainable business models. As investors plow money into growth, a new genre of subsidized business models emerges. This can have a profound impact on categories because a better experience is delivered to the consumer. The innovation is not the idea, it will have been thought of many times before but ruled out as uneconomic. The novelty is that investors are prepared to fund behavior change such that the consumer gets something for nothing. We are beginning to see many of the most publicized stories fail as there is no path to profitability and no sustainable value proposition or business model. These brands can be hard to salvage as they are often defined around benefits that are unsustainable. If you're going to build, build to last.

One of the greatest Founders of any generation is Jeff Bezos. Like many Founders, he has the clarity of purpose and business model that direct his company's development. "We've had three big ideas at Amazon that we've stuck with .... And they're the reason we're successful. Put the consumer first. Invent. And be patient." The rewards of investing in Amazon have been proven over time. What started as a subsidized model scaled, diversified and strengthened to one of the world's most profitable and valuable companies. Purpose driven from the start, passion and persistence fueled the innovation that created the progress to build a sustainable and scalable business.

Lessons from Founders are at the heart of what the industry needs in this new era. The business outlook is uncomfortable, dynamic, difficult and uncertain. Every business, big or small, must revisit its reason to be in the context of the new future. When you look through a Founder's lens everything seems possible. The scale of the journey becomes apparent. It becomes clear how much growth you have to be prepared for personally and in your team. Powered by purpose is easy to say. Making a difference with purpose is real pressure. You have to get comfortable with big ideas and big actions, with a passion to weather the challenges. You have to stay the course as there is no such thing as an overnight success. Progress takes time and persistence.

Yet when you commit to grow like a Founder, you commit to run your business for its potential not its past performance. That is a Founder's legacy. The power of building something is profound.

"Those who create are rare;
those who cannot are numerous."

Coco Chanel

BUILDERS WANTED.

CHAPTER SIX

TODAY'S BATTLEFIELD

The basic premise of this book is that we are likely to see more change in consumer goods in the next ten years than we have seen in the last two or three decades. Many understand the themes of change, but few have understood that the impacts are largely still to come. The trends are converging, which brings new scale to the consequences that will disrupt the market. Change will accelerate as legacy models begin to fail. Our markets will be fundamentally different in ten years' time.

Many companies lack a strategy, a strategist and a clear plan to deal with this future. They are still squeezing the last juice from the old playbook and using short-term tactics to delay the inevitable. Recognizing obsolescence in the old path to value is critical to shifting gears to the opportunity ahead. Drucker said, "The greatest danger in times of turbulence is not the turbulence, it is to act with yesterday's logic." The era of benchmarking and balance sheets had two significant consequences. Firstly, it could make the average look outstanding financially through inorganic (and effectively temporary) value creation levers. Secondly, benchmarking trained a generation of leaders to focus on being the same as everyone else. We lost the battle for USP to the pursuit of homogeneity and copy/paste cost playbooks.

We have two decades of institutionalized groupthink to shake off. The advisors that trained us to obsess about cost ratios have left us with the worst organic growth rates since the 1990s. Growth capabilities need to be rebuilt. We must restore aspiration, invention and differentiation. We must focus on true legacy thinking and go back to the Founder roots of our business, to rediscover the power of building something. We can be future ready and future proof by restoring business development to the front and center of our strategy. Committing to growth will force us to change at a pace equal to or greater than our customers and consumers.

The second half of this book paints a detailed picture of what is changing in our markets and what we will need to consider in our response. It introduces frameworks for developing your new strategy and executing with activity-based management. The book focuses on the mindsets as well as the methods of strategy, detailing the journey for the working team. It also explains the essential balance needed to make your new plans equally ambitious, implementable and affordable.

After all the interventions made in the value chain, we have designed a business model where competitive advantage sits almost entirely in the customer and consumer dimension of the brands we operate. Value creation will pivot around the impact we have with these stakeholders. There is much less cushion available from cost savings and balance sheets to compensate for weak brand activity. Indeed, winning in this new environment will often require dis-synergies and increased operating complexity.

We need to think deeply about the dynamic landscape and the forces at play in forming our strategy. The volatility of the marketplace will affect all players, and the winners will be those who best navigate the uncertainty. The future is about creating real opportunity from real change. There are three forces at work in the battlefield: channel discontinuities, evolving consumer behavior and the possibilities of technology.

Channel discontinuities are to a large extent a zero-sum game. They have more impact on where people buy than what and why they buy. Online growth will radically change the footprint and role of brick & mortar stores. Despite the headlines, this process has barely begun. The annual growth of online sales in dollars is now of a magnitude that will create significant consequence each and every year. Yet the percent of sales online still has room to more than triple from where it is today. The market will see a battle between eCommerce specialists, omni-channel winners and distressed store franchises. The economics of retail are marginal at the best of times. The expected level of disruption will polarize winners and losers.

Making our ideas matter more to the consumer is where we must turn to for growth. Deep consumer understanding that translates into innovation, high impact marketing and market development. This will be a three-way fight between large household names, insurgent brands and private label. The abundance of choice available in today's marketplaces, coupled with always-on digital demand creation, means the battle will play out in a crowded and cluttered environment. Cut-through and competitiveness is critical. Tactical ideas will be copied with lightning speed. Me-too mixes will be drowned out.

The third dimension, technology, sits alongside channel and consumer dynamics sits as a great enabler, accelerator and integrator of change. It will have a key role in demand creation, a new playbook of efficiencies and the optimization of value chains. An abundance of readily available technology is yet to be adopted in CPG. Long-term strategy will need to include the possibilities of technology being better integrated into business plans.

The analogy of the battlefield is helpful in describing not only the dynamic nature of the situation, but also two important aspects of change that all companies will face – marketplace dynamics and business model evolution. Business dynamics are akin to the individual battles of any campaign. There will be opportunities and threats to your market share and many protagonists on the field of battle. Meanwhile, your business model sets out how you plan to compete. Do you have the forces and equipment needed to win the campaign? Your new strategy must meet the demands of the volatile business dynamics while developing the business model needed to win in the 2020s.

There is a decade of disruption ahead. Decades of stable, entrenched market structures are giving way. Dedicate top talent to a deep strategy refresh rooted in how your markets will evolve. Work back from this perspective to create a roadmap for change. Position your business to win. Embrace what needs to be different. Execute with urgency and ambition. Pick a lane. Build a plan. Make it happen.

CHANNEL REVOLUTION.

CONSUMER EVOLUTION.

TECHNOLOGY INTEGRATION.

TODAY'S BATTLEFIELD

CHANNEL REVOLUTION

The major catalyst for many of the business dynamics we are seeing is the acceleration of online growth. Much of today's c-suite got its operating experience when eCommerce growth was just a few billion dollars a year and largely incremental. Today, that figure in the US is rapidly approaching $100bn of growth a year, every year. This is the equivalent of adding the whole Target franchise or two Best Buy's into the market every year. Sales are no longer mainly incremental and so a very large amount of demand is rotating. The eCommerce volume is often served by supply chains designed for the low complexity brick & mortar world and has sub-optimal economics as a result. Online sales today are 15-20% of the market depending on the definition used. Individual categories can be as high as 80-90% of sales online and many are 25-50%. It is highly likely that online penetration will triple in the next 10-20 years to around half of total sales. Each point of growth is equivalent to closing 8,500 physical stores.[1] Consumer durables have seen greater online penetration than FMCG categories, but all penetration curves are rising (quickly).

While "Retail Armageddon" gets more than a million hits on Google, the idea that store closures have already happened is entirely misplaced. This is all ahead of us. In a study of 1,660 US retail chains, 1,065 net opened stores in 2019. Only 12% of chains net closed stores and 75% of all store closings were done by just 20 companies.[2] We have continued to net open stores in the majority of retailers. The only format to materially downsize is Department and Specialty with nearly 10,000 stores closed since 2017. The US is potentially very over-stored as there are more than twice the number of stores as Europe on a comparable basis, despite the greater maturity of online in the US.[3]

Retail has always operated with tough economic constraints. The best retailers make about one-quarter the margin of the best suppliers. The weaker retailers make about one tenth of the margin of the weaker suppliers. In brick & mortar, high fixed costs mean that all profitability is contingent on the last few percent of foot traffic and the peak seasonal periods. Changing store footprints is a long-term and high-cost undertaking. That is why most retail innovation is only incremental until a new player opens with a blank canvas and fresh thinking. Changing from within is hard and expensive. Many retail franchises are struggling to remain relevant because they lack capacity for change. In 2015-2019 we saw about $50bn of retail bankruptcy liabilities, the majority in a few big names like Toys "R" Us. The fallout of COVID-19 is accelerating store closings, retail bankruptcies and online penetration.

The winners are investing hard. Amazon built to a larger valuation than Walmart in one-third of the time and was not trying to make any money at all from retail sales. Walmart spent more than $3bn on Jet as a catalyst to a new omni-channel business model. Many retailers are adapting their networks, using stores as a cost-effective way to fulfill online orders as they look to close the gap in eCommerce.

The market is quickly evolving into three cohorts of retailer. Online pureplay, omni-channel winners and distressed franchises. Each of these groups is being forced to be bolder and compete harder in the disruptive marketplace. They all have a great deal of marginal economics at risk. Retailers will be bold because they have to be. Standing still is not an option for any of them.

Online pureplay is beginning to bifurcate between highly complex marketplaces with unlimited assortment and a number of smaller curated platforms. The latter create calmer, immersive shopping experiences that help the consumer browse, and in some cases, offer additional benefits like personalization. Many brands are developing Direct to Consumer experiences in this vein as online can deliver differentiation and premiumization. In the marketplaces with unlimited ranging, an array of online merchants web scrape for ideas, source from industry suppliers and market and fulfill online. This is increasing competition and fragmenting market share, reducing industry profit pools. Business can be built with very little overhead and therefore run at lower margins than traditionally existed in the category. Outside partners help with fulfillment and demand creation on a variable cost basis.

The threat of online is causing many retailers to raise their game. The winners to date are clear. Mass omni-channel. Home Centers. Club. Discount and off-price. Competition is high and so each franchise is balancing specialization with heightened promotional activity. Many are investing heavily in online platforms and faster delivery or collection lead-times. Stores will become more experiential and offer immediate "one stop shop" solutions. 75% of consumers still enjoy going to a store and touching products.[4] Store assortments will likely evolve in response to where online penetration is highest and lowest.

The strategy of Drug and Grocery franchises is still a work in progress. Those formats have very high store counts and local proximity to the consumer. Their future propositions are not yet fully defined. It seems inevitable that Grocery will consolidate but also move further into the trends on buying local from regional craft suppliers and the local fulfillment for online sales. Drug is likely to shift towards services and a new category mix to use store footprints differently. There will likely be a lower dependency on impulse purchases of basic lines which rapidly convert to online replenishment and pantry loading. Aging populations and rising healthcare costs will foster innovation in healthcare technology and services, shaping drug store strategy.

The distressed group of retailers are made up of sub-scale franchises, the department and specialty channel and businesses that rely on multi-step points of distribution. Online is exploiting the inherent waste in these business models. Multi-step distributor models pass goods between customers before they get to the end consumer. Each step takes a piece of the pie at the consumer's expense. In one-step online, those economics are eliminated, and the savings can be passed on to the consumer. Department and specialty suffer because their high-cost model of associate advisers and wide store assortment is being replaced by peer reviews, detailed content and unlimited assortment online. The consumer is often happier with the online alternative and a lower price. 57% of shoppers now prefer to purchase without human interaction.[5] The high price points and margins of specialty channels are becoming obsolete, in favor of a cheaper alternative experience.

For CPG companies, these channel dynamics challenge their business model. As we plan ahead, we must recognize the winning customers will have more leverage than they used to. Brands will not be able to demand customer support, they will need to earn it. Those same customers will have a clear strategy for brands to align with and adapt to. Brands must create ideas big enough to develop the market and delight the consumer while adapting their agenda to the winning customers and channels. Implicit in this will be recognizing that the future may be quite different from the past. A deep understanding of channel evolution, and what it means for your footprint, will be critical. Shift the balance of your business towards the winning channels while optimizing declining channels and managing the demand shocks of potential bankruptcies, store closures and inventory impacts.

ECOMMERCE IS A P&L, NOT A PROJECT.

Many companies are still in the early stages of developing their eCommerce business model. Many didn't expect the level of change we have seen. In 2014 a survey of retail and consumer goods CEOs

"WE COULD GO AWAY AT ANY MINUTE. IF YOU'RE NOT WILLING TO FAIL, YOU'RE GOING TO GO AWAY."

–DOUG McMILLON

put the two smallest risks identified as "failing to sustain brick & mortar sales" and "failing to break the silos and integrate physical stores with eCommerce". Only 28% of CEOs thought these were even relevant challenges for their organization.[6] eCommerce is a new function for the enterprise. Different technology and systems, different analytics, different demand creation levers, different customer strategies, different packaging requirements and different value chain economics. It is not just different, it is fast. Opportunity is almost immediate, and lead-times are short. Forecasting is unpredictable as the demand curves are less well-established. Competition and complexity are significantly higher than they are for the core customer shelves. Much of the opportunity is in developing efficient operations while scaling revenue to full potential. The greater assortment gives much weaker shares to large brands online. Share consolidation of the top four players is about 1/3 lower online than in-store. Speed, agility and entrepreneurial leadership are key to the eCommerce organization. Jeff Bezos is famous for his Day One mindset at Amazon. The temptation will be to slow down progress with process and to use talent without eCommerce expertise to bring the operations closer to the core. Success in eCommerce means embracing the culture, ways of working and lead-times that are needed.

OMNI-CHANNEL STRATEGY

The larger the eCommerce P&L, the more important the interaction with the core business customers and the necessity of omni-channel thinking. Many corporations look at this back to front, trying to "fix" the traditional customers first and limiting eCommerce investment for its perceived threat to the core. This is King Canute stuff, resisting the irresistible. It frequently leads to over-investment in declining customers with short-term promotions and under-resourcing bets on the future. A robust and well thought through omni-channel strategy is key to any brand today. Act now. Chasing the winners will only get more expensive, and the cautious approach will likely result in lower market share and smaller profit pools. Over-planning distressed channels will create profit holes and potentially limit your investment in growth.

TODAY'S BATTLEFIELD

CONSUMER EVOLUTION

The business dynamics with the consumer are much more evolutionary than what we see in the channel landscape. Many of the shifts in purchasing behavior are fostered by the changes in retail. Online has transformed choice. Marketplaces offer unlimited assortment. Products can come to market in weeks, not years. It's faster and cheaper to gain placement and build awareness with the consumer than it has ever been. Advertising can be consumed continuously in a seamless blur of digital, social and traditional media as well as influence by peers and endorsers. It's now affordable to reach the customer and consumer, even for small brands.

This has created the battle of the brands. Insurgents are achieving significantly accretive growth rates and price points. The dynamic of choice is here to stay. Since insurgents have driven all the category growth for retailers, they are getting more attention than the big brands. The big brands launch by far the most activity and spend the most money, but with almost no incrementality to the category. As retailers become more confident in driving traffic without relying on the large traditional media spends and promotional budgets of big brands the shift towards smaller brands and wider choice could accelerate further.

While the aggregate impact of insurgents is big, the level of success achieved by many tells a different story. There is more clutter than cut-through. Par market share for a mass brand would typically be about 3% to have sustainable levels of awareness, trial and repeat, and an economic model that supports investment in advertising and innovation. Almost all insurgents fail to achieve even 1% share in their category. Many are losing share. Initial trial often doesn't lead to repeat sales. Too much focus on the look and feel of a product can mask underlying efficacy issues. In some cases, return rates are well beyond product recall levels on larger brands. Propositions are often focused on niches limiting volume potential. Distribution is often concentrated in a few lead customers and performance may not merit wider availability. There is a great deal of churn and relatively few examples of progress. This is a major missed opportunity as the stage is set for insurgents, but many have rushed for quick wins, especially online. Few have taken the time to craft the proposition, product and high performing mix to create a scalable platform.

It is not clear that today's insurgents will survive a fight back from big companies. Many insurgents will either mature to stronger business models or disappear. The big brands have to be

"IT'S ALRIGHT TO BE GOLIATH, BUT ALWAYS ACT LIKE DAVID."

–PHIL KNIGHT

better at what they do to fight back. Competing on tactical levels plays to their weakness as smaller brands have better incremental economics. Brands must use their scale to advantage instead. Faster decision making, bolder innovation and communicating the advantages they have built from years of investment in product and consumer understanding. Meanwhile, there is a significant threat from the healthy and growing equity in many retailer brands. Seven of the top-25 American brands are retailers. Only five are CPG manufacturers' brands.[7] Retailer brands like Amazon and Kirkland have scale as large as the major CPG holding companies. Few leading retailers have maximized their potential to innovate or deploy a good/better/best private label strategy. They cover much less of the market than the consumer would embrace. This could change. Small insurgent brands have much less equity than the retail brands that could replace them. Rationally, this is what should happen after many insurgents failed to perform. This battle of the brands has many twists and turns still to come, and there is profound opportunity for the winners.

As we look to reignite growth, the next question on consumer dynamics is how to build plans around changing consumer trends. While there are many variables, there are no individual dynamics big enough to move the needle. Consumer goods is traditionally a pretty stable universe. Category preference drivers are slow to shift, and there is little evidence of major changes in recent years. Much has been made of millennial consumers and the difficulties of reaching them. Like insurgent brands, much of this wisdom is taking facts out of context and not looking holistically. It is true that Millennials embody the wider changes in society that have been in flight for decades. It is a much more multi-cultural generation with greater ethnic, religious and racial diversity.[8] It is also a generation where more people go to college, so there is more student debt.[9] There's an aging population, so we are all faced with rising healthcare costs and inadequate pensions. The young feel that in their paycheck more than wealthier, older consumers. We are all shopping online more. We are all watching less cable TV and streaming more. We are all working in companies for less tenure than we used to.

To the degree Millennials are different to other cohorts, some things may surprise you. They value brands more than any other age group. They look for product performance and category benefits above anything else in their purchasing decision. They are slightly more cause-oriented than other cohorts, but this is a tertiary preference driver for all. While they are disproportionately trusting of big brands, they like to do their own extensive research taking recommendation from multiple sources with relatively equal weighting. They like to buy remotely without a lot of human interaction. Price is less of a driver of their purchase decisions than it is for older consumers.

For global brands the most important differences are between markets rather than between age cohorts. Secondly, the trends that impact all cohorts are more significant than the differences between cohorts. Third, (and last) is the differences between cohorts. So, don't be distracted by Millennials or generational thinking in isolation, pay attention to the underlying trends with large scale impact.

The dynamics of how brands reach the consumer are changing.

Traditional media has continued to grow and get more expensive because it offers the reach that big brands need. Around 85% of US consumers of all age groups are more likely to trust a new product from a brand they know.[10] Awareness and reach still have great value. After 20 years of scaling, digital advertising platforms are now beginning to achieve reach comparable to traditional media. This will be powerful when combined with their capabilities in targeting and interactive engagement.

The evolution of advertising is still early in application of data, personalization and programmatic buying. Millennials and Gen Z are more brand centric than older consumers. They stream more and watch less live TV, although very little advertising has so far moved to streaming. Millennials consume more ads across all channels than other age groups. Peer recommendations and personal experience have significantly more influence than any other tactic.[10] Influencers are the least influential communication tactic with millennials.

Digital and social media are the most crowded spaces which inevitably makes it difficult to be heard. We have started to value noise and PR above changing behavior in advertising. New messages are created little and often, sometimes out of cadence with the story the brand has to tell. By fragmenting both medium and message, no critical mass is built in any one campaign or channel. Many brand managers also fail to define the role of each medium. We celebrate the quantum of impressions and not the impact on sales. Advertising should not be judged on entertainment value or recall; it should be judged on its impact on behavior. Did people purchase the right brand for the right reasons after seeing the ad?

THE CONSUMER IS BOSS.

While I don't believe there are more than evolutionary business dynamics at play, the business model challenges are quite significant. That's because we have operated for much of the last 20 years in a manner that was inconsistent with these dynamics. Cost savings were placed ahead of the consumer. Many brands lightened formulations, reduced innovation and relied instead on tactical sales levers. With the benefit of hindsight, several of the decisions on portfolio simplification and complexity reduction were a mistake. They did not take account of the explosion of choice that online would foster. The savings achieved in supply chains will be a fraction of the lost gross margin on lost sales for many companies.

Complexity is a source of profit pools online, and there are many variable cost partners to help handle the operational challenges. Weakening the core business model at the same time as barriers to entry were falling was the wrong choice. Large companies created space for insurgents. They will now face years of higher cost of competition. Meanwhile, few have seized the full potential of online and as a result, online shares are substantially more fragmented than the brick & mortar stores they are replacing. That means profit pools are lower. Brands that resisted the potential of online created the space for others to take their place.

The consequences of a generation of inward thinking created a hubris that delighting the consumer and customer didn't matter as much as delighting the shareholder. The business model needed to win hasn't changed, but the bar for the winners has been raised – competition is higher, and the winning customers are stronger.

Millennial and Gen Z consumers are the most diverse and informed of any generation to date. They trust in brands, but they have the tools and opportunity to get what they want, when and where they want it. They won't be denied this choice and expect brands to earn their loyalty through understanding and answering their needs. Theorists will say this is the same as any generation, but in practice the entrenched market structures of the past prevented the level of choice we are now seeing. Power has shifted to the consumer through the scale and universality of online. Always on, always available.

THE CHALLENGES OF SCALING ARE SET AGAINST THE CHALLENGES OF SCALE.

The need to strengthen consumer impact in marketing is critical to both insurgents and mature brands. There is too much clutter and too much derivative activity. Profit pools will either atomize across tertiary brands with limited business models or the winners will invest to win share and cut-through. The opportunity to lead share consolidation is open to all players. It is challenging to grow from a smaller start, but incremental economics help fuel you. Larger brands have the advantage of scale and experience but only if they put it to work meaningfully. The winning formula is the same for all brands. Well-defined and differentiated propositions based on consumer understanding. Portfolio management that builds equity in key brands while increasing coverage of the consumer map. Innovation that brings news and heightens competitive advantage. Thoughtful expansion into new categories and countries. High impact marketing that is good enough to change behavior. We must look at the world through consumers' eyes and design to be better. Cut-through, in all aspects, will be critical to success. Fragmentation abounds in many brand tactics which fosters both inefficiency and ineffectiveness. Too often, tactics and high frequency, low impact activity detract and distract from what really moves the needle. That is why it is so important to measure the consumer impact of all that you do.

TODAY'S BATTLEFIELD

TECHNOLOGY INTEGRATION

The battlefield will pivot on the consumer and customer variables that I have outlined. Technology will act as a catalyst for both and present solutions to many of the business model challenges. While many consumer products may be similar to those that our grandparents used, the same is certainly not true of the technology that pervades our life at home, at work and at leisure. Technology has been a foundation of innovation and value chain efficiencies. There are multiple dimensions in which technology will be a strategic driver in the coming years. It will often be technology built outside consumer products that can be adopted into the industry as an efficient and effective way to speed up progress. There are three broad areas where technology is likely to be more fully integrated into strategy.

DEMAND CREATION

The adoption of technology into our core products is seriously underdeveloped. There are some challenges that constrain this pace of adoption. It is a simple truth that you make more money from a dying old technology than from a new one. It makes financial sense to keep as much of the old analog business for as long as possible. New technology by contrast can be risky, expensive and slow to scale. The possibilities new technology affords should push us beyond these initial constraints. Technology delivers the kind of disruptive innovation that step-changes core product benefit delivery. New technology intersects directly with wider trends like convenience, on-the-go, connectedness, smart homes and eCommerce.

Consumers are looking for more personalized choice. Delivering tailored value becomes a real possibility from the combined rise of technologies like ambient computing, identity detection, rapid small-scale manufacturing and pervasive 5G connectivity. We are looking towards a world where potentially every in-store, online and physical interaction with products becomes custom tailored to provide as much (or little) personalization as consumers want. Individual blends of flavors, formulations and sizes. Unique information display, customized specials and in-store experiences. Products, interfaces, and environments can be situationally aware and able to respond to consumer and shopper emotion. Commerce will be frictionless as shoppers transact with far fewer (if any) clicks as shopping systems work in the background, presenting opportunities to connect with brands only when maximally relevant. The barriers from consideration to purchase become increasingly small when the store is instantly available without diverting attention from the point of inspiration. It's these kinds of applied technologies that will catalyze new growth on consumer and channel dimensions.

VALUE CHAIN OPTIMIZATION

The cost cutting and outsourcing playbook of the last 20 years may have largely run its course, but the opportunity to use technology to create a new generation of efficiencies is all ahead of us. Technology can help us manage the cost of complexity. This will enable more relevant choices for the consumer and locally optimized mixes for the retailer, at attractive margins for the supplier. Manufacturers will likely be forced to adapt to greater ranging, smaller batch sizes and a faster pace of innovation. Mass production and homogeneity will be a smaller part of the markets than it was in the last 20 years. New approaches to production and distribution, made feasible by new technology are required to manage this complexity at scale.

Technology is a major part of the solution to the biggest challenges we face as a society. Solving the problems of sustainable business as we seek to make more and better things using less of the world's resources. Helping us tackle sustainable living, rising population and income inequality. Technology is likely to be key to new supply chain and manufacturing solutions, making global marketplaces ever more efficient and using data, product and process innovation to reduce waste and develop more intelligent consumption habits.

Technology will also help optimize the omni-channel supply chain. Data rich chains of custody create much tighter controls over origin and material history. They create fluid systems of supply rather than linear chains. This minimizes inventory and builds resilience against unforeseen events. Ranges of new technologies in logistics, transportation and distribution networks are evolving together to address the dis-synergies of eCommerce. Advanced inventory tracking, localized warehousing, automated pick, pull, pack, freight and last mile logistics shrink eCommerce response times and increase flexibility.

POWERING ORGANIZATION PRODUCTIVITY

There's a full range of machine enabled processes on the horizon that may wholly transform the nature of work. Impacts well beyond manufacturing and industrial processes will accelerate human productivity in the fourth industrial revolution. We're seeing it first in AI driven discoveries in pharma, but these same approaches in the abstract may transition quickly to the business space. Employees will use management-friendly predictive modeling and AI applications in their everyday work as seamlessly as email and desktop publishing now. The goal will be to shift the raw data to the background, highlighting only the relevant synthesis and recommendations for human interaction. Brand and channel teams will have far more evidence to back bold moves and far greater understanding of potential scenarios.

The management of massively complex data to inform decision making will increase. Pulling and analyzing data from across the value chain will become commonplace. Real time inventory, store level stocking levels, shelf sets, and supply chain data all interconnect to address supply chain challenges. Much deeper and more immediate understanding of demand will be possible. Forensic consumer understanding and predictive models of behavior will become mainstream.

TODAY'S BATTLEFIELD

REAL CHANGE IS COMING

"In times of change learners inherit the earth; while the learned find themselves beautifully equipped to deal with a world that no longer exists".
– Eric Hoffer

The clichés say change is always an opportunity. The message of this book is slightly different. I simply say real change is now upon us. We've been fairly sheltered to date, but now the forces of stability are giving way to the forces of change. That's my point. You decide how to react but think carefully. The way we made money in the past, the business model we pursued and the conditions that created stability for our markets are all changing. The challenge is profound to the maintenance teams with "cash cow + credit" plans and calendar year focus. It's just not going to cut it anymore. This model was, and will be, tremendously successful right up until the point it isn't. Then it will begin to unravel, and a cost cutting spiral to plug earnings holes will begin. Every business has a different starting position, I cannot tell you exactly where your breaking point will be. I can tell you that your pivot point must come well ahead of that if you are to control your own destiny and reposition early enough to succeed in this fast-changing market.

My best advice? I urge you to make sure that the assumptions underpinning the business plans of the next decade are not the same as those from the last. The market dynamics are different and the business model needed to win is different. You must then ask yourself what these new assumptions really mean for your business footprint, your portfolio priorities and the capabilities you need to win. You cannot cut your way to success. You will need to be able to re-imagine and re-engineer your operations for what matters going forward.

The battlefield is set around the consumer and customer. The key to success is managing your impact on these two dimensions. The balance of power has shifted. Brands need to earn their keep. Customers have big decisions to make to ensure they can survive the channel revolution that is underway. Aligning your brand agenda to the winning retailers is critical to commercial success. Consumers have responded to heightened choice and welcome innovation. Loyalty will need to be earned. Homogeneity will be replaced by "right for me." Technology can make a lot of the change possible and profitable.

The gap between winners and losers is going to increase. Capacity to change will define the winners.

MY CENTER IS GIVING WAY, MY RIGHT IS IN RETREAT; SITUATION EXCELLENT.

I SHALL ATTACK.

-GENERAL FERDINAND FOCH

CHAPTER SEVEN

DEVELOPING TRANSFORMATIVE STRATEGY

While the 2020s bring a great many challenges, they will also be the canvas on which business architects do some of their finest work. Leaders who can build will be in great demand. Now is a time to embrace change and create opportunity from it.

Your new strategy must pivot your footprint to the winning customers and channels. You must recognize that there will be significant disruption in established routes to market and that these dynamics are only just beginning to work through. You will accept that some channels require new business models to be efficient, and you'll design towards that. The greatest progress will be made when customer and brand strategy genuinely intersect. Brands that develop categories will be in demand from customers because of how well they delight the consumer. Timeless marketing strategy disciplines must guide us through the dazzling array of available tactics. Consumer impact is possible when everything is rooted in deep understanding of the consumer. Technology will be an accelerator of both growth and efficiencies and play a greater role in value creation.

There is change needed in our business plans to adapt to the new business dynamics. There's a need to rebuild our business models for the new reality. Barriers to entry are lower, competition is higher, the pressures on customer partners are formidable and complexity is pervasive in assortment choice and marketing media. This is not a time for business as usual. Use refreshed strategy to determine and direct your response to all variables.

The balance of this book lays out frameworks for the methods, mindsets and implementation of strategy. These are integrated ideas to help you navigate through a complete process. The threads of the book are distilled into frameworks you can act upon. Robust strategy is thorough. Effective strategy is balanced. Transformative strategy is made so by investment in change management.

BRINGING BALANCE TO STRATEGY

Almost every strategy exercise I have ever seen begins with heightened ambition. The numbers must always go up. Whether it's a turnaround problem needing a fix or a fast-growing brand looking for its full potential, the expectation is always the same. Bigger and better. This is a positive dynamic for encouraging fresh thinking, but to be realistic it forces a focus on balance in your final plan. Balance is what will earn you the time and space to change the course of your business. Expecting too much too quickly will defeat any strategy.

You effectively have four levers to trade-off, and you are looking to maximize overall results. The process starts with your financial objectives and stakeholder expectations. This is usually a mixture of new ambition and some initial direction, coupled with constraints on financials and the level of risk that can be taken. From here you look to identify the major moves that will drive the key changes you are looking for. In principle these priorities must get what they need to succeed. In practice their commercial delivery must be realistically measured and sequenced.

The new priorities will need capability development in the team to be successful. This takes investment of money and time to nurture change. Having identified new investment in your business priorities, you now need to look to the base business and find paths to make it fundamentally more efficient. There are many levers available to a decisive team. This process should be entrepreneurial – focusing on

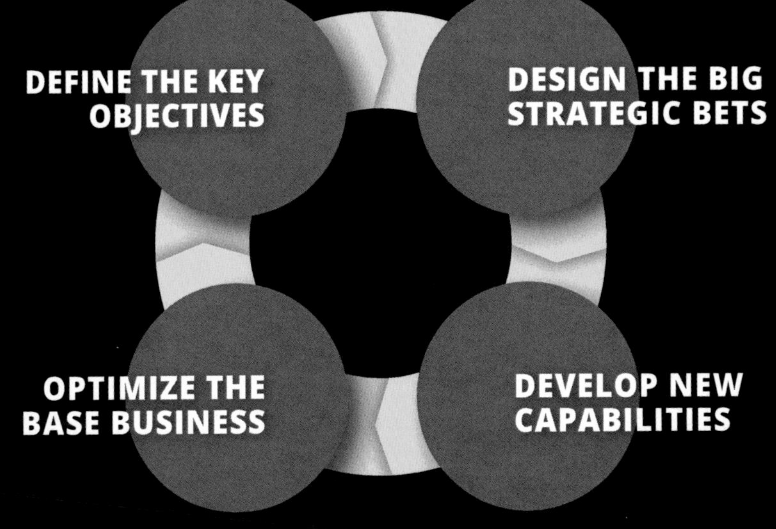

$ profit contribution rather than optimizing % margins. The key is to use levers that have high probability of success and high certainty of outcome. These initiatives anchor the funding your strategy needs. This is an iterative process. There are multiple variables. How many things you try to do, and how far and how fast you try to progress. The team must find the right path to balance the strategy. This is critical to being able to bring consistency to the organization, which is how big things are achieved. An unbalanced plan results in stop start dynamics. Once you are behind plan, it gets very tempting to revert to short term management, and the strategy is often abandoned. By contrast if you design the right amount of change in a credible cadence you can make continuous progress and your course corrections should be modest.

THE MINDSETS OF STRATEGY

I have learned over the years that a disciplined process for strategy helps make the work more rigorous. However, when I look back at the most successful teams, I don't remember the process used, I remember the way the teams approached the task. Mindsets are what make any method work. A holistic process is both left brain and right brain. Logic and magic. Enough rigor to root ideas in facts and to follow significance. Yet you wouldn't be starting the exercise if a linear extrapolation of your results was adequate. So you need creativity and fresh thinking. The process is iterative. Teams diverge as they develop ideas and eventually converge on a final plan. Balancing the plan takes tough choices and prioritization. The method helps the team navigate through the necessary steps. The mindset is what makes the difference.

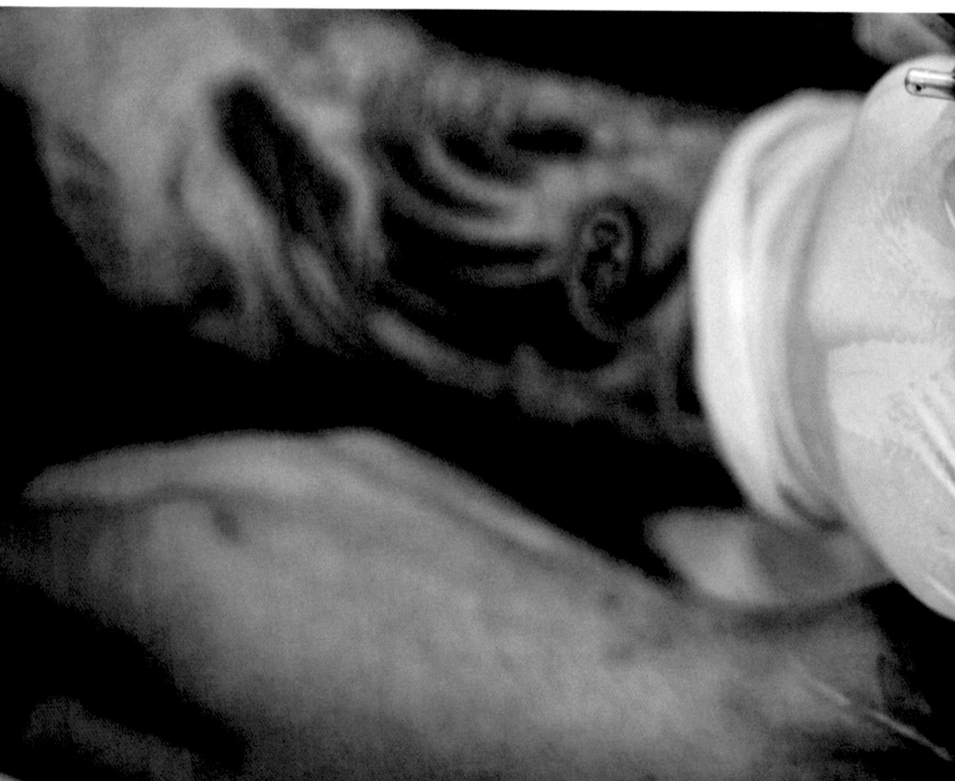

The team works through four mindset phases. Two left brain, two right brain. Immersion, imagination, choices and change.

The first is immersion, which is looking at everything de nova, particularly the drivers of change in your markets. Follow the facts not opinions. Next comes imagination. Build from the immersion phase into ways to act on what you have learned and create new opportunity. This creativity is unconstrained. You have to think big, and you have to think beyond today's business. Next comes choices. A plan full of dreams will not achieve your goals. Choices are about rational prioritization of ideas and understanding the implications of those ideas to pick those that are attractive and actionable. Finally, it all becomes about change management. Developing your organization, culture and ways of working to deliver the full possibilities of your new strategy.

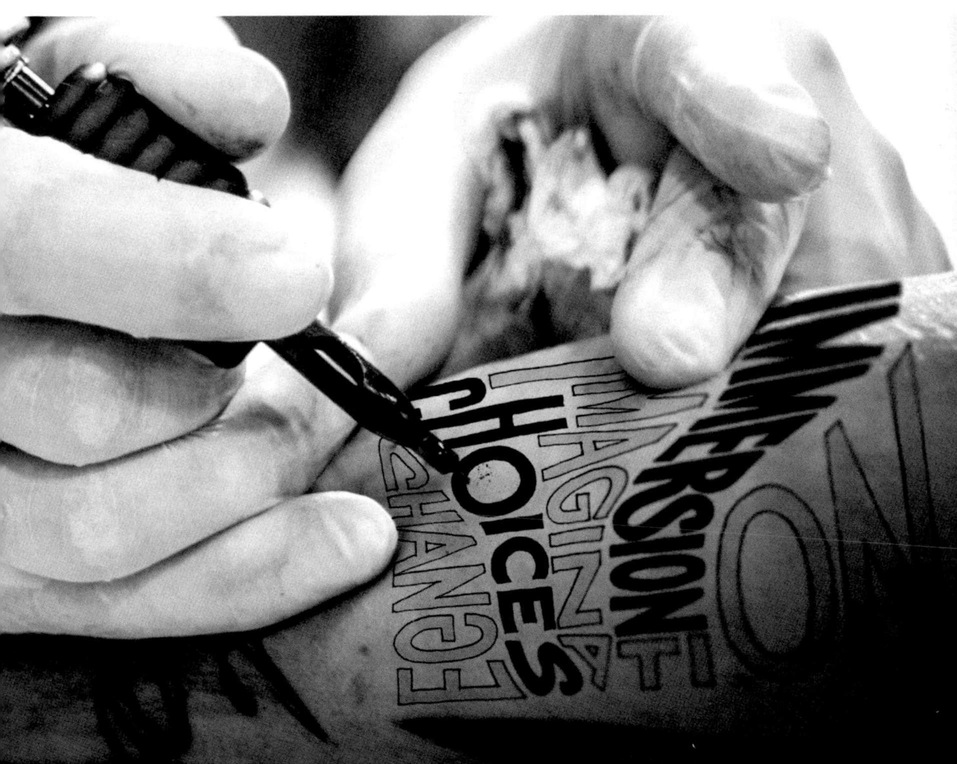

THE METHODS OF STRATEGY

The mindsets weave through a 6-step strategy process that I have developed over many years. The steps are outlined in detail in the rest of this chapter. Before this, I wanted to share some observations from experience that may help you in any form of strategy process.

The first is that strategy is not for delegation. If you are committed to make serious change in your business, you want your best people to design it. The achievers. A full strategy review is a big time commitment but, at the same time, nothing is potentially more important to your business.

Secondly, the process needs grounding in your market dynamics and some facts, but it can't be biased by the things you can easily measure. You use your best people because you trust their judgment and experience. There is no such thing as strategy from a spreadsheet. Competitive advantage now sits in the intersection of your management of consumers and customers. The working team should reflect this, and the exercise should not be prisoner to Finance or Corporate. Process should be in service to progress.

Thirdly, the 6-step process reaches all the way into communication and change management. There is a great tendency to disband strategy teams as soon as the PowerPoint summary is done. Great strategy is developed with a complete process and focus over time, not a couple of off-sites and straight back to the day job. The most important stage is in detailing the change needed to action the new plans. An objective appraisal of the capabilities and resources you have today and what you will need to be successful.

The temptation to operate at a thematic level and not objectively confront this issue hinders execution more than anything else I have seen.

Finally, the quality of organization engagement will make all the difference to execution. Ideas are not enough. The way the strategy comes out of the working team and gets the organization enthused about the new potential and changes required is worthy of deep thought. You have new priorities, new ideas to action and new capabilities to build. The path forward is exciting, but the potential of the strategy is in the broader business. So many plans end up in the drawer. What we are looking for is the new multi-year roadmap and the path forward that allows everyone to make their best contribution to the future. Invest deeply in communicating and sharing your plans.

At the start of this book I said strategy is not execution. Instead, I believe something else. That what matters with strategy is what you actually execute. Those are very different ideas. Don't shortcut the process, much is riding on the quality of the work and more importantly what you then do with it. Committing to a strategy process is committing to fundamental change.

The **MINDSETS** and **METHODS** of Strategy

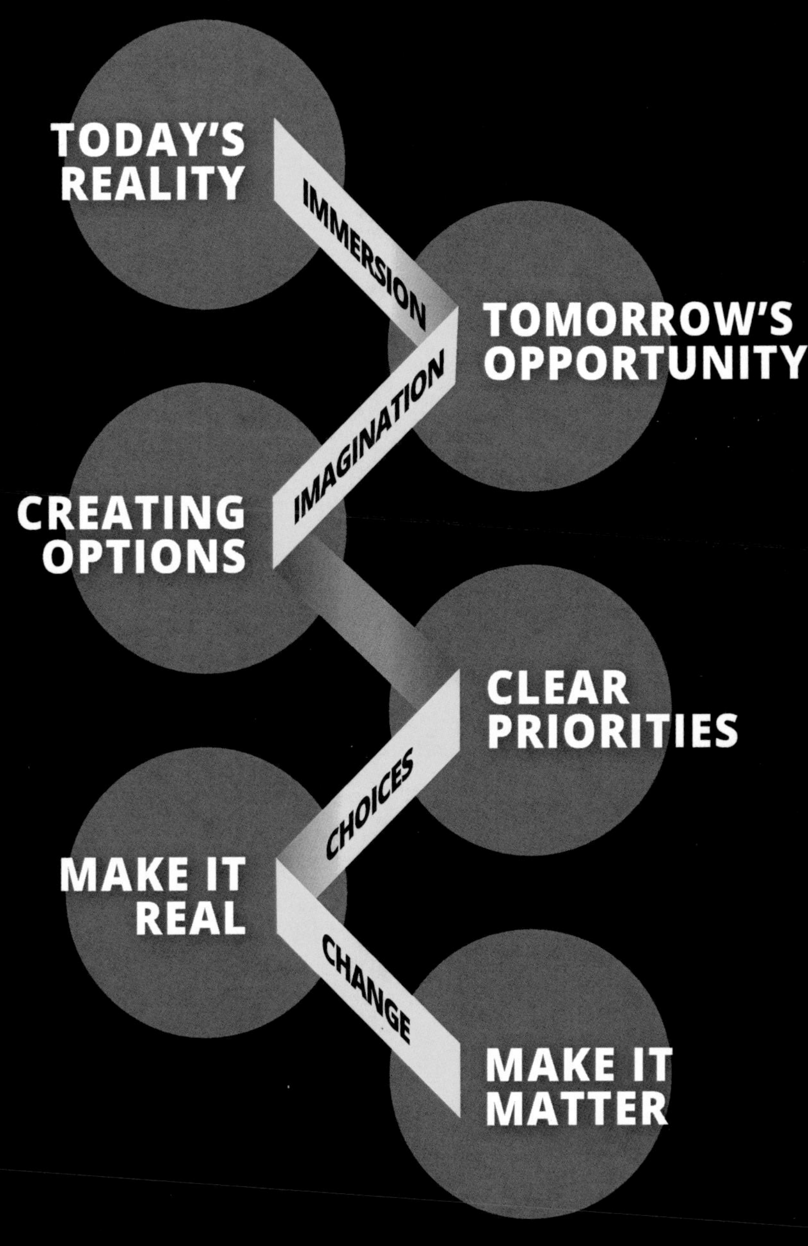
TODAY'S
REALITY
IMMERSION
TOMORROW'S
OPPORTUNITY
IMAGINATION
CREATING
OPTIONS
CLEAR
PRIORITIES
CHOICES
MAKE IT
REAL
CHANGE
MAKE IT
MATTER

1

TODAY'S REALITY

RUTHLESS OBJECTIVITY ON THE BASELINE

**"Make it simple,
but significant."**
– Don Draper

Build a comprehensive and highly visual fact-base of historic trends and current performance. Pictures and stories that help a cross-functional team immerse themselves in the business. Internal and external data. By looking at a broad set of information you get a holistic and objective picture of the starting point for the strategy. This should be reviewed in the context of the objectives required by your stakeholders. Compliment this with initial discussions with the team. What choices have we made historically and why? What is holding us back? Summarize the first thoughts on major opportunities and challenges for the strategy to address.

2

TOMORROW'S OPPORTUNITY
REIMAGINING YOUR BUSINESS EVOLUTION

"Don't bunt. Aim out of the ballpark. Aim for the company of immortals."
– David Ogilvy

Use stimulus and facilitated working sessions on key trends and industry dynamics to scenario plan how the customer and consumer landscape will change. The team has to explore the opportunities and threats, but without being constrained by today's business. This is the opportunity to look at the longer term and beyond linear thinking that dominates most short-term business plans. Look to find the few key catalysts that have the potential to shape your future business. Understand them in enough detail and quantification to identify implications for building your business. At this stage, there may be several alternative paths to pursue and choices are not yet required.

3

CREATING OPTIONS
DEFINING YOUR MAJOR MOVES

"Nothing is worth doing unless the consequences may be serious."
– George Bernard Shaw

This is the time to tangibly develop the big strategic thrusts. Ideas should be grounded in the work to date to ensure their relevance and objectivity. What are the main elements of the new strategy? Ideation techniques from product development are often helpful to the process. This strategizing phase is the critical test for your team. They must think beyond today's boundaries and be Founders of the next generation of ideas. The implications of each move should be understood and significant. There must be adequate coverage of the opportunities and threats identified to ensure the strategy has balance and sufficient impact. This means a blend of portfolio strategy, growth initiatives, capability development and efficiencies.

4

CLEAR PRIORITIES

MAKING THE MAIN THING THE MAIN THING

"Business is often about killing your favorite children to allow others to succeed."
– John Harvey-Jones

There are only so many moves you can afford to make. We are constrained by resources, risk profile and time. The unconstrained strategizing process is followed by hard choices to get to a plan that adds up and optimizes the total business. Quantify the ideas in terms of time, cost and difficulty. Then rank and sequence them. Remove any conflicts. Disciplined prioritization and resource allocation are the "genius bar" of strategy. It is how you learn how to make the strategy really work. Real prioritization should make it painfully clear what has to be given up. The harder this is, the more real it is. The team should emerge with an outlined new strategy that crystallizes what is going to be different and how.

5

MAKE IT REAL
NEW OPERATING PLANS

"The way to get started is to quit talking and start doing."
– Walt Disney

The output of making choices should give each business area a new brief with a specific set of expectations and actions. Each operating team should then be asked to lay out a detailed, costed plan to implement the new strategy. My view is this is best done in a 3-year time horizon with first year mile markers set. The leadership team should review the new plans diligently. The work should include stopping or repurposing legacy activity to ensure all resources and programs align to the new choices. Do not back off the big choices at this pivotal moment. Organizational democracy can suffocate great strategy. Recidivists will bite back. They'll resist the reallocation of resources and the consequences of the new priorities. The strategy must optimize the total business, not individual pieces. You made your choices with this in mind. Stick to them. They will unlock the change that will get you the results you aspire to.

6

MAKE IT MATTER
LET THE TEAM THRIVE

**"I could either watch it happen
or be part of it."**
– Elon Musk

The last step is the most important in making a difference to execution. This is when you create operational clarity on what is going to be different and build energy in the team for the future of the business. I use one-page strategies to create a communication vehicle that can be used across an organization. Leaders should create interactive and consistent engagement on the new strategy. Use the new strategy to create catalysts for change that the team can embrace and contribute to. Done well, the communication of a clear strategy creates the freedom for imaginative execution. Leaders will often find that far more is possible, far more quickly, once the organization is engaged. Designing and implementing change programs to develop the new capabilities required can allow the team to grow with the business. Maintaining energy, focus and consistency on the drivers of the new strategy will enable great execution.

CHAPTER EIGHT

STRATEGY INTO ACTION

The 6-step process laid out the methods and mindsets you'll need to develop and launch your new strategy. This is the start of a multi-year journey. Real change needs persistent focus and investment, sustained energy and commitment. Strategy into action must become the day job, not just a special project. Too often in business, strategy stalls in the face of short-term disruptions which divert attention to incremental fixes. The bolder your plans, the more time and space you need to nurture the new activities. Transformation takes time. Stay focused. Stay the course.

Strategy into action requires balance in your business plans. Design a portfolio of activity to span across time horizons, risk levels and business levers. You must have activity upstream and downstream to impact all time horizons. You must have growth investments and new efficiencies. You must develop some disruptive ideas but also need to sustain a competitive level of easier, affordable incremental initiatives. You'll need to address all three of the business evolution variables: channel revolution, consumer evolution and technology integration. This is a multi-year effort. You cannot control all the external variables, but you can force a point of view on the future and design programs to position yourself for that outcome. As reality bites, you can subtly course correct, confident that your broad direction is well founded and funded.

Activity-based management is an effective way to move strategy into action. It gives you the framework to stop and start initiatives, reallocate resources, and continuously measure and manage your progress. Your operating rhythm, organization design and KPIs all flow from your strategy. In its simplest form, activity-based management allows you to check that your activities add up to your goals. This sounds obvious, but you'd be surprised how many businesses fail to measure what's important. Resource-hungry areas such as innovation are often not documented, validated or prioritized. In management reviews, aggregated financials often dominate conversations. Only the top most exciting initiatives are given airtime. There is often little clarity on activities beyond the immediate short-term plans. Assessing the plan in its entirety is nigh on impossible.

In the future, commercial success will depend on the intersection of customer and consumer impact. This is a new level of integrated business planning, aligning national brand activity to increasingly differentiated channel strategies. Recognizing that there will be substantial and continuous change in the channel landscape. Winners and losers will polarize. Navigating the moving parts while at the same time strengthening the quality of your plans is no small endeavor. This is why strategic clarity is so important as an anchor to how you deploy your resources and assess your operating plans. You will have to tackle a number of planning biases as you execute your plans. There will be a tendency to over-promise in the declining areas of the portfolio. Meanwhile chasing the winning customers too quickly or opportunistically may be financially unattractive. Fragmentation of brand activity is a great source of waste and is often hidden beneath the higher profile activities.

Despite all the noise, you mustn't lose sight of the important goals. Increasing the consumer impact of your brand activity is central to cut-through in categories that now have substantially more competition and a constant stream of new entrants. At the same time, you need to reposition to the winning channels of the future, even as you optimize your legacy business.

The following framework will help you map and assess your portfolio of activity on the critical customer and consumer dimensions. It's a dynamic tool to pressure test actual projects against your marketplace dynamics. It will help you navigate legacy and test your pace of change.

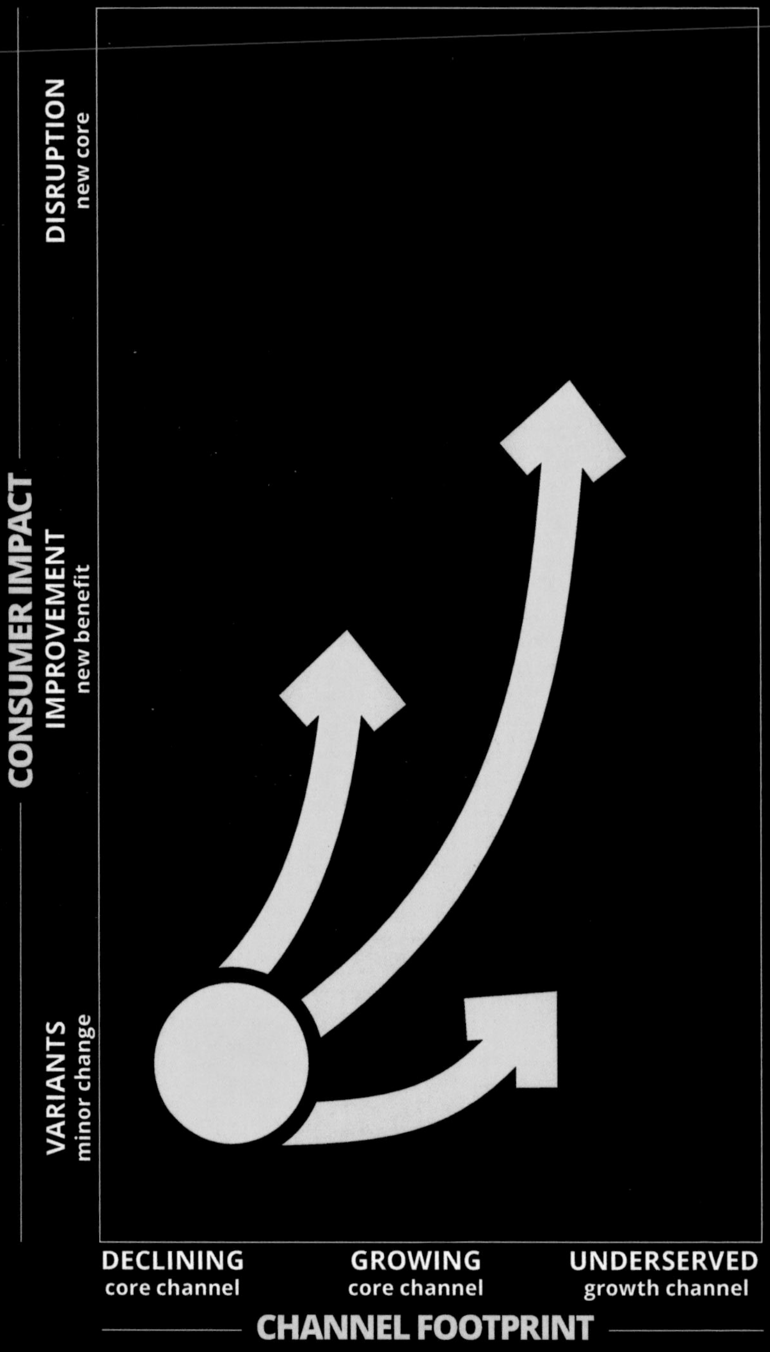

CONSUMER IMPACT

DISRUPTION
new core

IMPROVEMENT
new benefit

VARIANTS
minor change

DECLINING
core channel

GROWING
core channel

UNDERSERVED
growth channel

CHANNEL FOOTPRINT

GROWTH MATRIX
ACTIVITY-BASED MANAGEMENT

Your strategy should aim to create specific activities that widen your exposure to the growth opportunities in your markets. Through consistent investment in targeted initiatives, it will be possible to shift the weight of your business over time.

REPOSITIONING YOUR CHANNEL FOOTPRINT

The first dimension is to build market share in the faster growing channels. Start with your core channels and, over time, fill out blind spots in underserved growth channels. Adapt investments and priorities according to the long-term channel potential. Measure the % of your business in declining, growing and underserved channels. Make assumptions about channel shifts and quantify activity-based plans to meet your overall objectives and build your market position. Your choices should be ambitious, but with a phased approach and realistic expectations of results.

STRENGTHENING CONSUMER IMPACT

The second dimension is to strengthen activity with the consumer. A surplus of derivative, incremental activity fills operating plans and exhausts budgets. Your strategy must select fewer, bigger initiatives that are validated with the consumer. Higher impact activity spreads across levers and lead-times. A mix of selective long-term disruptive investments balances with a steady flow of meaningful innovation, renovation and brand expansion into new categories. A finite amount of simple to execute derivative and promotional activity balances the plan.

FOUR PHASES OF ACTIVITY
MANAGING A PORTFOLIO OF PROJECTS

Developing a multi-year strategy gives you a consistent context in which to make all your operating decisions. Change always has to be sequenced and funded to be successful. Strategy into action done well builds on your starting point. Don't try to go forwards by going backwards first. This is one of the most common mistakes. Teams intervene on one piece of the puzzle without balancing the consequences elsewhere. The plan should always move you in the right direction towards your overall goals. It's a set of chess moves, one by one. Neither all-out attack nor defense will win.

There are four phases to working with the growth matrix. First, implement your priorities and some basic interventions to get more from the core and move activity towards the future. Legacy operations that have been deprioritized can often be made more efficient. Act on this at the same time as creating positive offsets in the growth priorities. In the first 6-18 months, impactful growth accelerator programs can be developed. Manage this with detailed project management and make sure the interventions balance risk and reward. At the same time, begin creating the future, setting resources to work on high impact innovation and brand expansion. There is a lot you can achieve in 18-36 months. Seed the disruptive moves. These are high risk, but potentially high reward breakthroughs. Give the initiatives time and space to succeed. Ensure the projects are scalable and have the potential to move the needle. Ensure they are consistently fundable to nurture progress.

4. DISRUPTIVE BREAKTHROUGHS

The most challenging space in the matrix. It inevitably goes beyond the current boundaries of the brand and business model. The best approach is thoughtful, steady exploration. Projects should progress selectively and with a research-rich development process. Scalability is necessary to justify investment. Partners or M&A can help speed progress.

3. CREATING THE FUTURE

This is where you commit to significantly expanding your brands. Major innovations, adjacent categories, new geographies and, very selectively, new brand launches. These are big commitments, not tactical initiatives. They should not be attempted unless they can be consistently funded over the time it takes to change consumer behavior.

2. GROWTH ACCELERATORS

Quick wins will refocus your team and give your stakeholders reasons to believe. Don't delay increasing funding for your best mixes that can still be scaled further. Do first what you do best. Be imaginative on ways to create incremental contribution from lower priority brands, eCommerce and new investment in growth channels.

1. MORE FROM THE CORE

Creating capacity for change is crucial. Resources need to be freed up to invest into the growth drivers. Intervene on the lower priority areas. Change the amount of legacy activity, reallocate investment and, over time, change organization design and business model complexity. Cutting the tail of activity can give you a head start.

DECLINING core channel	GROWING core channel	UNDERSERVED growth channel

CHANNEL FOOTPRINT

DISRUPTION
new core

IMPROVEMENT
new benefit

VARIANTS
minor change

CONSUMER IMPACT

Technology rich innovation

Growth M&A

Selective new geographies

Selective category adjacencies

International eCommerce

step change CORE INNOVATION

DTC

$ eCommerce business model development

Rapid renovation and increased spend on strongest mixes

Full potential eCommerce plan

$ optimize contribution of bleeders... channels/brands

$ Maximize distribution on full portfolio

$$ Reallocate resources to priorities substantial reduction in legacy activity. Optimize organization around the strategy.

DECLINING
core channel

GROWING
core channel

UNDERSERVED
growth channel

CHANNEL FOOTPRINT

PLANNING YOUR MOVES
THE TACTICS BOARD

Activity-based management is very much like the coach's tactics board. There is a big picture which allows leaders to look at the size and shape of projects on the field of play. Are there enough interventions to reposition for growth? Do we have enough efficiency projects to create the funds we need? Do we have enough safe plays to balance the potentially game-changing moves?

You can map measurements to this tactics board. Measure your channel footprint and how it is evolving. Map where you are spending your money and ask if the dollars match up to the potential. Assess whether you have a good balance of short- and long-term investment. As examples, map your innovation funnel according to its consumer impact, quantify your eCommerce footprint development, and plan for the offsets in other channels.

This is an operators framework. Rather than simply study financial reports and PowerPoint Promises in business reviews, align your operating rhythm to activity-based management. For each brand, map your activity and your spend. Compare the grid to the objectives for that business and see where you need to intervene and close gaps. The power is in working continuously with the framework. Plan and make moves. That's strategy into action.

This is a practitioner's strategy book. I have not included academic theory or case study thinking. Rather these are tricks of the trade developed over many years in different types of business. They are intended to help you see the path to the solution, but also to remind you that change comes from within. How you work together as a team and how much time you put in to designing your new strategy will make all the difference. The strategy process empowers you to be anything you want to be. It helps you work through the consequences of your ambitions, so that your plan adds up and meets your stakeholder requirements. The growth matrix is all about a philosophy of management that change comes from doing specific things differently. We should treat growth and strategy into action as a measurable project, just like we manage our supply chain or cost savings programs.

Strategy becomes real when the ambition of the ideas phase is carried forward into determined execution. When your team actively designs a new operating rhythm, KPIs and ways of managing legacy business. When they are fully committed to the new possibilities that come from the new strategy.

A changing environment is not a reason to fail, it is a reason to make new moves. It's reason to accept that what got you to here may not be what you need in the future. It's a reason to take the initiative and not let events overwhelm you. Create the conditions for change and you create the conditions for success.

"PEOPLE ARE ALWAYS BLAMING THEIR CIRCUMSTANCES FOR WHAT THEY ARE.

I DON'T BELIEVE IN CIRCUMSTANCES.

THE PEOPLE WHO GET ON IN THIS WORLD ARE THE PEOPLE WHO GET UP AND LOOK FOR THE CIRCUMSTANCES THEY WANT, AND IF THEY CAN'T FIND THEM, MAKE THEM."

-GEORGE BERNARD SHAW

CHAPTER NINE

FINAL THOUGHTS

The trigger for writing this book was a 20-year low in organic growth. Despite all the winners, the rise of insurgents and the development of eCommerce, there is barely any aggregate growth at all in mature markets. This is definitive proof that we haven't yet adapted to the changing market conditions. For larger companies, it is evidence that twenty years of cost savings have left a profound legacy. There is too much internal focus, short-termism and tactical emphasis in today's business plans. Our ability to look up, look out and look forward has been diminished. There is an abundance of activity but a scarcity of impact. From the perspective of our customers and consumers, our plans often aren't good enough.

The dominant theme of this book has been that you should expect the future to be different to the past. Prepare for it, plan for it and act on it. Real change is now upon us and it is accelerating.

PICK A LANE.
BUILD A PLAN.
MAKE IT HAPPEN.

We know a lot about this new future. It is highly likely that we will get less value creation from financial levers, and we will need to rely more on organic performance. It is highly likely that cost savings will fall unless we embrace new ways of doing business and adopt new technology. It is highly likely that the decades-long pattern of customer and consumer stability will give way to a new landscape with more consumer choice, stronger winning customers and, unfortunately, many of the weaker customers facing store closures and financial problems.

Many businesses don't have a strategist nor, more importantly, a strategy. I have tried to show the dangers in this approach. In a rapidly changing world, the worst thing to do is stand still. In the old world simply sustaining performance created value. Indeed, for large profitable firms, this may have been all your stakeholders wanted so long as your profits kept going up. The danger in dynamic markets is that when you try to stand still you will actually get left behind. Winning customers will not carry passive or passenger brands. The consumer has an abundance of choice, available almost instantly, and will no longer compromise in the same way as they were forced to when only a few customers and suppliers ran the show. The danger is many businesses will pivot too late from focusing on profits to profitable growth. I wonder how many will look back at this period and wish they had embraced change firmer and faster.

I have worked with and talked to a great many businesses in recent years. I've seen a prevalence of tactical solutions to strategic problems. The curse of incrementalism. Larger brands cannot conceive how they can compete harder against insurgents with lower margin expectations, lower costs and more agile business models. The problem is they are looking for a quick fix in a calendar year business plan. A strategic approach would give them the opportunity to convert scale to advantage with customers and consumers, and mobilize their greater resources. This may sometimes require shifting constraints on the legacy business model. At the same time insurgents, flushed with the success of a flurry of sales with one or two customers, are overly optimistic about their potential. The up and coming digital-centric agencies they work with lack deep branding expertise. They focus on brand look and feel executions, but without the fundamentals of proposition and a scalable point of difference. A triumph of style over substance. The weak performance of many insurgents leaves the door open for retailers to build private label instead. The battle of the brands has a long way to run.

I have talked a lot about what we can learn from Founders. Purpose, perseverance and passion that fuels progress. The courage to grow through every challenge that is overcome. Brands of all sizes can learn from these stories. Having the patience and business model to sustain investment and focus is key to any big idea coming to reality. There are few overnight successes, and yet so many put most of their energy, investment and execution in short-term business plans. What you can achieve in all aspects of growth through consistency of purpose is profound. What you can't do is add short-term tactics together to create a long-term strategy. I have tried not to skim over the reprogramming many businesses need. The world of 30 years ago, when a lot of value was held in physical assets, is gone. Value chains have converged. Outsourcing has reduced our ability to differentiate. The world where barriers to entry were high, with entrenched distribution and high cost of advertising, is also long gone. Online sales and digital demand creation changed all of that. Today, competitive advantage is held almost exclusively in brands and customer relationships. Sustaining that advantage is about how you delight the customer and the consumer. Yet, so much of what we did in the era of benchmarking and balance sheets was in spite of the customer and the consumer, rather than in service to them. We must throw off the shackles of the cost savings era and focus our attention on building back differentiation into our core business model. Restoring consumer and customer impact will not be easy. Many of today's marketing teams have been trained in the cost savings era. They may never have launched a new brand, learned portfolio management skills or developed high impact innovation. Instead they may be overly skilled in short-term tactics and act as project managers rather than creators. At the same time, revenue in eCommerce is often ahead of the maturity of the business model. Inefficiency results because eCommerce is often being managed in a legacy brick & mortar supply chain.

The polarization of performance in retail and the pressures that flow from online growth will make the customer and channel dimension as important to success as the consumer dimension. Building national consumer plans and expecting all customers to execute in the same way is not going to work as it did in the past. Marketers will need to design channel strategy with meaningful differentiation into their plans. The winning customers will be demanding and the losers will be decisive. The intersection of brand and customer strategy is key to value. Insurgent brands face the same challenge, but from the opposite end of the spectrum. They must find the path to scaling out of their initial lead customers into national distribution. This requires careful crafting and will be dependent on their ability to establish repeat purchase with the consumer. The universality of online brings transparency to all tactics which is why I encourage deliberately designed business plans that connect high impact consumer activity with the demands and interests of high value channels. The growth matrix can help you operationalize this approach.

Strategy only matters to the degree it is implemented. Throughout this book I am urging you to respond strategically with the end in mind, not tactically with incremental fixes. Strategy into action means managing a portfolio of projects that balance risks, resources, time horizons and organization capabilities. You need to make enough moves to make a difference. You need to be methodical so that you make as many of the right moves as you can. You need to build your team as well as your business. You need to change your capacity to change.

The essence of 2020s strategy will be managing your business activity for impact on the customer and consumer grid. The major focus of the 6-step strategy process is to determine where, when and how you will compete. To understand what will change and to design opportunity from it. The growth matrix is all about establishing a culture and operating rhythm of activity-based management. Manage what you measure, establish a portfolio of activities. You need to create the space, resources and rewards to balance short-term results with investment in longer term ideas. You need to create the conditions for leaders to commit to multi-year business development rather than be rewarded for changing jobs in 2-3 year cycles. Founder -led businesses have a philosophical advantage here as they have a longer-term perspective than public companies where even CEOs have tenure of only 5-6 years.

Change comes from within. Asking your top talent to define the future path of the business is a big undertaking. The mindsets of strategy are as important as the methods. Immersion in the past, present and potential of the business. Unconstrained imagination to think through the possibilities. Sharp choices that truly make the main thing, the main thing. Funding the priorities fully and first. Optimizing the whole so that it is greater than the sum of the parts. Finally, commitment to deep change. The power of building something with your team and helping them grow.

These mindsets will not only create a strategy. They will be the foundation of a shift in your culture to pursue ideas big enough to reposition your business and develop your team to its full potential. If your goals are ambitious enough, it will not all be plain sailing. Just like the story of Sistema's manufacturing journey, the growth required will be exponential. Commitment to change means commitment to try difficult things that might fail. Then to persevere and try again. Michael Jordan said, "I've missed more than 9,000 shots in my career. I've lost almost 300 games. 26 times, I've been trusted to take the game winning shot and missed. I've failed over and over and over again in my life. And that is why I succeed."

The winners are going to be defined by their ability to embrace change. Steady state management will be second best. It's not going to be a close second. You can be as methodical and disciplined about growth as you are about any other aspect of your operations. Manage what you measure and be the champion of activity-based management. De-risk and differentiate your ideas by basing them on a deep understanding of the consumer and customer. Use balance in your strategy to create the conditions for stability and to manage variation in results. Reward builders and reward outcomes. Build your strategy, team, culture and goals around winning.

Use this extraordinary environment as a catalyst for change and a source of new opportunity. Set a clear and consistent direction and act on it. Work to get better at execution every day. Leverage consistency of purpose to build the team. That's how you get ahead and stay ahead.

Now is not a time for incrementalism. Be bold. As Sir Alex Ferguson once said, "I never played for a draw in my life."

ABOUT THE AUTHOR

Mark has over two decades experience in consumer goods. He is a rare c-suite strategist and is deeply experienced in designing and executing growth programs on brands of all sizes. Mark was global Head of Strategy at Unilever and launched the Compass strategy. In 2011 he founded a strategy agency which he later sold to Newell Rubbermaid having created the Growth Game Plan. He was Chief Development Officer at Newell Rubbermaid from 2013 and President of Newell Brands from 2015. Mark led all of the company's growth functions including marketing, design and innovation, eCommerce and corporate development. Mark quit corporate life in the spring of 2018 to pursue an entrepreneurial career as an advisor and co-investor in brands with significant growth ambitions. He works with a talented team of growth executives based in the U.S. and Europe. Mark lives in Manhattan with his wife Catherine and two very spoiled cats.

NOTES

CHAPTER 1

1. Gartner, 2020. "Gartner Quarterly Update on Top Emerging Business Risk". https://www.gartner.com/smarterwithgartner/gartner-quarterly-update-top-emerging-business-risk/

CHAPTER 2

1. Ocean Tomo, 2015. "Annual Study of Intangible Asset Market Value from Ocean Tomo, LLC". https://www.oceantomo.com/media-center-item/annual-study-of-intangible-asset-market-value-from-ocean-tomo-llc/

CHAPTER 3

1. Harvard Business School Publishing, 2019. "Rewiring Modern Organizations for Adaptability and Continuous Change". https://428v733jwynp2jhljs12i1h8-wpengine.netdna-ssl.com/wp-content/uploads/2019/11/HBR_Survey.pdf

2. Nasdaq, 2019. Letter from John A. Zecca, Nasdaq, Inc. to the SEC. https://www.sec.gov/comments/s7-26-18/s72618-5825362-187511.pdf

3. Challenger, Gray & Christmas, Inc., 2020. "2019 Year-End CEO Report", 2020. http://www.challengergray.com/press/press-releases/2019-year-end-ceo-report-160-ceos-out-december-highest-annual-quarterly-totals

4. SpencerStuart, 2019. "Chief Marketing Officer Average Tenure Drops to 43 Months". https://www.spencerstuart.com/research-and-insight/chief-marketing-officer-average-tenure-drops-to-43-months

5. McKinsey & Co, 2019. "The next wave of consumer M&A: Searching for growth". https://www.mckinsey.com/industries/consumer-packaged-goods/our-insights/the-next-wave-of-consumer-m-and-a-searching-for-growth

6. Credit Suisse, 2019. "Shareholder Activism: an evolving challenge". https://www.credit-suisse.com/media/assets/microsite/docs/corporate-insights/shareholder-activism-an-evolving-challenge.pdf

Image Credit: Imperial War Museum, 1940. "Winston Churchill studies after action reports with Vice Admiral Sir Bertram Ramsay, 28 August 1940." Public domain. https://commons.wikimedia.org/wiki/File:Winston_Churchill_studies_after_action_reports_with_Vice_Admiral_Sir_Bertram_Ramsay,_Flag_Officer_Comanding_Dover,_28_August_1940._H3508.jpg

CHAPTER 4

1. Nasdaq, 2019. Letter from John A. Zecca, Nasdaq, Inc. to the SEC. https://www.sec.gov/comments/s7-26-18/s72618-5825362-187511.pdf

Image Credit: Robert Roe, 2020. "Fighter". Original work used with permission. Reference image, "Muhammad Ali fights Brian London on August 6, 1966". Public Domain. https://commons.wikimedia.org/wiki/File:Muhammad_Ali_fights_Brian_London_on_August_6,_1966.jpg. Source image, "

CHAPTER 5

1. Willis Towers Watson, 2019. "S&P 1500 pay-for-performance update: 2018 incentive plan payouts trend above target". https://www.willistowerswatson.com/en-US/Insights/2019/07/S-P-1500-pay-for-performance-update-2018-incentive-plan-payouts-trend-above-target

Image Credit: Robert Roe, 2020. "Contractor". Original work used with permission. Reference image Golstejin, Marion, 2014. "Afbeelding van Coco Chanel tijdens de tentoonstelling Chanel:De Legende in het Gemeentemuseum Den Haag". Creative Commons (CC3). https://commons.wikimedia.org/wiki/File:Coco_Chanel_tentoonstelling.JPG

Image Credit: mostafa_meraji, 2020. "Construction build amerneia yerevan". Public domain (CC0). https://pixabay.com/photos/construction-build-armenia-yerevan-4939383/

CHAPTER 6

1. UBS Report, 2019. https://www.businessinsider.com/retail-apocalypse-thousands-store-closures-predicted-2019-4

2. IHL Group, 2019. "Retail Renaissance". https://www.ihlservices.com/product/retails-renaissance/

3. Kantar Retail IQ, 2020.

4. Deloitte, 2019. "The consumer is changing, but not perhaps how you think". https://www2.deloitte.com/us/en/insights/industry/retail-distribution/the-consumer-is-changing.html

5. Whistl Study, 2018. https://internetretailing.net/mobile-theme/mobile-theme/who-needs-humans-half-of-shoppers-prefer-to-use-self-checkouts--18383

6. PwC on behalf of JDA Software, 2014. "Global Retail & Consumer Goods CEO Survey". http://now.jda.com/rs/jdasoftware/images/PWCExecutiveSummary_D.PDF

7. 2017 Annual Reports

8. Pew Research Center, 2018. "How Millennials today compare with their grandparents 50 years ago". https://www.pewresearch.org/fact-tank/2018/03/16/how-millennials-compare-with-their-grandparents/

9. Pew Research Center, 2019. "Millennial life: How young adulthood today compares with prior generations". https://www.pewsocialtrends.org/essay/millennial-life-how-young-adulthood-today-compares-with-prior-generations/

10. IPSOS, 2017. "Millennial Myths & Realities". https://www.ipsos.com/sites/default/files/2017-07/Ipsos%20-%20Millennial%20Myths%20and%20Realities.pdf

Image Credit: Nationaal Archief, 1918. "Maarschalk Ferdinand Foch (1851-1929)." Public domain (CC0). https://commons.wikimedia.org/wiki/File:Maarschalk_Ferdinand_Foch_(1851-1929),_Bestanddeelnr_158-1095_(cropped).jpg

Made in the USA
Middletown, DE
22 August 2020

16290247R00084